Commodore 64 Disk Systems and Printers

Other Granada books for Commodore 64 users

Business Systems on the Commodore 64
Susan Curran and Margaret Norman
0 246 12422 9

Commodore 64 Computing
Ian Sinclair
0 246 12030 4

The Commodore 64 Games Book
Owen Bishop
0 246 12258 7

Commodore 64 Graphics and Sound
Steven Money
0 246 12342 7

Software 64: Practical Programs for the Commodore 64
Owen Bishop
0 246 12266 8

Introducing Commodore 64 Machine Code
Ian Sinclair
0 246 12338 9

40 Educational Games for the Commodore 64
Vince Apps
0 246 12318 4

Adventure Games for the Commodore 64
A. J. Bradbury
0 246 124121

Commodore 64 Disk Systems and Printers

Ian Sinclair

GRANADA

London Toronto Sydney New York

Granada Technical Books
Granada Publishing Ltd
8 Grafton Street, London W1X 3LA

First published in Great Britain by
Granada Publishing 1984

British Library Cataloguing in Publication Data
Sinclair, Ian R.
Commodore 64 disk systems and printers.
1. Commodore 64 (Computer)   2. Data disk
drives   3. Printers (Data processing systems)
I. Title
001.64′4   QA76.8.C64

ISBN 0-246-12409-1

Typeset by V & M Graphics Ltd, Aylesbury, Bucks
Printed and bound in Great Britain by
Mackays of Chatham, Kent

Contents

Preface   vii

1   About Disks and Disk Systems   1

2   The Disk Filing System   13

3   Digging Deeper   25

4   Disk Utilities and How To Use Them   35

5   BASIC Filing Techniques   43

6   A Database Example – FILING CABINET   63

7   Printers   77

Appendix A: Random Access Files   97

Appendix B: List of Commands   100

Appendix C: Disk Head Care   104

Appendix D: Word Processing with a Disk System   106

Appendix E: Saving Machine Code as a Serial File   108

Appendix F: Suppliers   110

Index   113

Preface

At some time or another, a serious programmer will find that the use of cassettes is intolerable, and will turn to disk drives. Since the memory size of the Commodore 64 machine makes it attractive to serious programmers, it is inevitable that a very large proportion of C'64 users have acquired, are acquiring, or intend to acquire disk systems. The Commodore disk system, however, is unique, and its operation is not obvious to a beginner. Even an experienced programmer who has worked with other disk systems may find that the Commodore 1541 is by no means easy to understand.

This book is intended as a beginner's introduction to the Commodore 1541 disk system that is currently available for the C'64 machine. By 'beginner' I don't necessarily mean a beginner to the use of the computer, but a beginner to the use of disk systems. At the same time, I hope that this book will be intelligible and useful to the beginner who has launched into computing with a disk-equipped Commodore 64. The main feature of this book, then, will be greatly extended explanations of what disk operation is about, and how to make the most effective use of disks. This is not always apparent to the newcomer to disk systems, even after considerable experience of the use of the cassette-based machine. I shall not assume, as so many books on disk operation seem to assume, that the reader is at ease with machine code or hexadecimal notation, so these points will be explained as they are introduced.

The book also covers the use of some 'disk utilities' – programs (usually supplied on disk) which can provide editing actions for disks. Listings of some of these utilities are provided in the 1541 manual. The beginner generally finds the action of these utilities very confusing, and so I have included some examples of how such utilities can be of very great help – for example, in reading data from a disk and in retitling a disk without removing its contents.

Since the serious programmer is quite certain to wish to use a printer, a long chapter on printers has been included. Only one of the Commodore printers, the VIC 1515, has been included, because the Commodore owner who uses a Commodore printer is generally well-served for advice. The important topic that is not so well covered in other texts is the use of non-Commodore printers, such as the Epson series. The use of a Centronics interface for the C'64 is described, and also the action of printers such as the Epson, the Juki daisywheel printer and the Tandy CGP-115 graphics printer. At a time when combined typewriter/printers can now be obtained at very attractive prices the buyer should have as wide a choice as possible, and this book describes what is available and how it can be used.

The listings in this book have, as usual, been prepared by a printer linked directly to the computer. This has made it impossible to reproduce Commodore graphics symbols, so that all of the functions (like clear screen) which are usually shown on listings as symbols are in this book typed in CHR$(n) form. This makes the listings very much easier to follow.

As always, this book owes its creation to a number of people. I would particularly like to thank my long-suffering and patient friends at Granada Publishing. Richard Miles commissioned the manuscript, and Tony Palmer detected a need for the book. As always, Sue Moore did miracles on my typescript, and the typesetters and printers worked at breakneck speed to bring the book quickly into existence. I am deeply grateful to all of them.

Note: The spelling 'disk' has been used throughout the text of this book. This is the U.S. spelling, which has become universal. A few texts, however, use the alternative 'disc'.

Ian Sinclair

Chapter One
About Disks and Disk Systems

Why use disks?

One of the questions that a beginner to computing inevitably asks is: Why use disks? The obvious reasons are not necessarily the most important ones. The novice owner will see more clearly the advantages of using disks only after some time spent using cassettes. We'll start, then, by showing why the use of disks is so important for the more advanced programmer and user. To start with, a disk offers much faster operation. If you use a machine to load one program, and then use that program (a game perhaps) for several hours, this speed advantage may be of little use. It certainly would not justify the cost of a disk system. On the other hand, if you are developing programs for yourself, you may want to load a program, make changes, and save it again before you try the new version out. This can be very tedious if you have to wait for cassettes to load and save. It's made even more tedious because cassette operation is not automatic. You either have to store each version of the program on a new cassette, or use a long cassette (C60 or C90) with each program version noted as a starting point on the tape counter. If you use separate cassettes, you may find yourself holding a dozen of them by the time the program is complete. If you use C90s you will need paper to note the tape count positions of each version of the program. Either way, it's tedious. Another class of user who will benefit greatly from the use of disks is the text writer. If you use the Commodore 64, as many users do, to create and edit text, with the EASY SCRIPT or VIZA WRITE text editor programs, then the time that is needed for cassettes to load or save the data is a definite handicap. If you want to load a piece of text, change a few words, and then store the new version back, the loading and saving time is a very large part of the total.

The overwhelming advantage of using a disk system is automatic operation. The C'64 cassette system does, at least, permit the motor of the cassette recorder to be controlled, and it allows programs or data files to be referred to by name. If you try to load a program called "TEXTINDEX", however, without winding the cassette back to the beginning, you may find that the program cannot be loaded. This is because recording on tape is *serial* – you start recording at the beginning of the tape, and wind it on to the end. If you then want to load something which is at the start of the tape, you have to rewind it for yourself. The computer does not control the actions of fast forward and reverse, because the cassette recorder was never intended as a way of storing computer programs and data. The disk system, by contrast, is completely computer-controlled. The only manual action is that of putting in the correct disk, and making sure that it is the right way round. On loading, the computer will then use its disk operating system to find the program or other material that you want, from its title. Having located the start, it will then load the data into the computer in a time of a few seconds. Saving is just as automatic. The SAVE command is followed by a filename (and other information in some cases), and pressing RETURN carries out the actions of finding unused space on the disk and saving the data. The automatic nature of this action also means that a 'catalogue' can be kept on the disk itself. You can insert a disk and obtain information on what is stored on it without the need to play back the whole disk. Though you can also find the names of programs on a cassette, you have to replay a whole cassette to see its catalogue.

In addition to these compelling reasons for using disks, we must add the extra commands that the disk operating system permits. Some computers go much further in this respect, so that their disk system adds a BASIC of its own. In the C'64 disk system, the new commands are all closely tied to the use of the disk system itself, and we shall examine them in detail. Several of the extra commands, however, allow you to obtain a lot more information about how the data is stored on the disk. This will not be of immediate use to you if you haven't used disks before, but its usefulness will be apparent before long.

Finally, the use of disks can bring order and reliability to what can otherwise be a very haphazard business. When you use cassettes for filing programs and data you inevitably end up with a very large number of cassettes, all of which have to be catalogued. I had over two hundred cassettes at one stage! It can take a considerable time to locate a program, on a cassette. Although a disk cannot hold quite as much information as a C90 cassette, the information is much easier to get at. This encourages you to use the whole of a disk, whereas you might use only the first ten minutes of a C90 cassette. It's quite possible to find, for example, that you can keep all of the programs that you want to use on one single disk! This in itself is such a liberation that it almost justifies the use of disks by itself. Disks are slim and compact to store, so that a box of ten disks, holding a huge number of programs, will take up little more space than a couple of cassettes. The reliability of disk recording means that you can make a backup copy of a valuable program and be fairly certain that you will never need it. Unless you spill coffee all over a disk, demagnetise it or tear it apart, it's unlikely that you will lose a program. Cassettes are *never* so reliable.

What is a disk system?

'Disk system' is the name that is given to a complicated combination of hardware and software. Hardware means the equipment in boxes, software is programming which can be on disk or in the form of chips that plug into the machine. A disk system comprises the disk drive (or drives), the disk controlling circuits, and the disk operating system. The unique feature of the Commodore disk system is that all of these parts of the disk system are contained in the one box, the *disk drive box*. The disk drive is, in fact, a miniature computer in its own right, complete with its own memory. The drive is linked to the Commodore 64 by means of the data cable which is provided. This terminates in six-pin plugs at each end. There are two sockets on the disk drive, and the data connection is made by plugging one end of the cable into the socket on the computer (the socket next to the place where the cassette unit plugs in). The other end of the cable can go into either of the sockets on the disk drive. If you then want to connect a VIC 1515 or similar Commodore printer, it can plug into the other socket on the disk drive.

The disk drive should come with a mains cable to which a plug has already been connected. If this has not been done, Fig. 1.1 shows how this plug should be connected. It's preferable to plug this into the same source of power as the computer, so a four-way socket strip, as illustrated in Fig. 1.2, will be very useful to you. This allows sockets for the C'64, the disk drive, a monitor and a printer.

The controlling circuits for the disk system are in the form of circuits which are all contained within the disk drive unit, along with

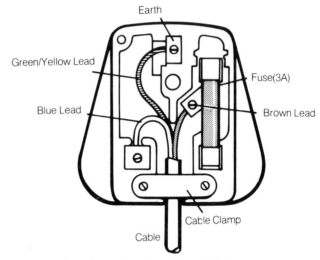

Earth

Green/Yellow Lead

Blue Lead

Fuse(3A)

Brown Lead

Cable Clamp

Cable

Fig. 1.1. Connecting the mains plug. Use a 3A fuse, not the 13A fuse that is supplied with the plug.

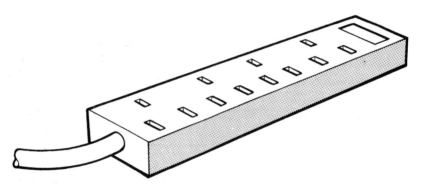

Fig. 1.2. A four-way socket strip that allows you to operate a complete system from one wall-socket.

the *disk filing system* (DFS). A 'file' in this sense means any collection of data which can be stored on the disk. The DFS consists of a program, and most computers use a 'DOS-disk' to hold this program. DOS is short for *disk operating system*. When this is done, a lot of the RAM memory (the memory that is free for you to use) is needed for holding the DFS. The Commodore 64, however, uses another chip, the DFS chip, to hold this information, and this leaves all of the memory of the C'64 free. Some memory has to be used, and this is fitted to the disk drive unit so that none of the 39K of the C'64 that is normally available to you for BASIC programs need to be taken up when the disk system is used.

Tracks, sectors and density

The language of disk recording is very different from that of cassette recording. If your sole concern is to save and load programs in BASIC, you may possibly never need to know much about these terms. A working knowledge of how disk storage operates, however, is useful. To start with, it can clear up the problem of which disks are suitable for your drives. At a more advanced level, it can allow you to extract information from damaged disks, and to make changes to the information that is stored on disks.

Unlike tape, which is pulled past a recording/replay head, a disk spins around its centre. When you insert a disk into a drive it is located in place, and when the drive operates a hub engages the central hole of the disk, clamps it, and starts to spin it at a speed of about 300 revolutions per minute. The disk is a circular, flat piece of plastic which has been coated with magnetic material. It is enclosed in a cardboard (or plastic) jacket to reduce the chances of damage to its surface. The hub part of the disk should also be reinforced to avoid damage when it is gripped by the drive. The surface of each disk is smooth and flat, and any physical damage, such as a fingerprint or a scratch, can cause loss of recorded data. The jacket has slots and holes cut into it so that the disk drive can touch the disk at the correct places.

Through a slot that is cut in the jacket (Fig. 1.3), the head of the disk drive can touch the surface of the disk. This head is a tiny electromagnet, and it is used both for writing data and for reading. When the head writes data, electrical signals through the coils of wire in the head cause changes of magnetism. These in turn magnetise the disk surface. When the head is used for reading, the changing magnetism of the disk as it turns causes electrical signals to be generated in the coils of wire. This recording and replaying action is very similar to that of the cassette recorder, with one important difference. The cassette recorder was never designed to record digital signals from computers, but the disk head is. The reliability of recording on a disk is therefore very much better than you can ever hope for from a cassette.

Unlike the head of a cassette recorder, which does not move once it is in contact with the tape, the head of a disk drive moves quite a lot. If the head is held steady, the spinning disk will allow a circular strip of the magnetic material to be affected by the head. By moving the head in and out, to and from the centre of the disk, the drive can make contact with different circular strips of the disk. These strips

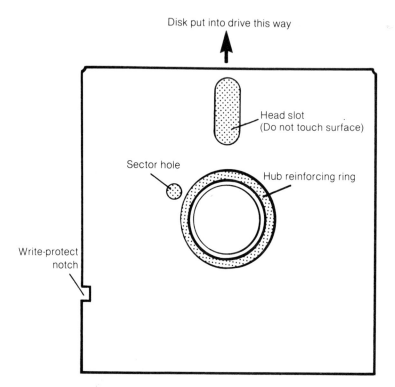

Fig. 1.3. The slit in the disk jacket that allows the disk drive head to touch the disk surface.

are called 'tracks'. Unlike the groove of a conventional record, these are circular, not spiral, and they are not grooves cut into the disk. The track is invisible, just as the recording on a tape is invisible. What creates the tracks is the movement of the recording/replay head of the disk drive. A rather similar situation is the choice of twin-track or four-track on cassette tapes. The same tape can be recorded with two or four tracks, depending on the heads that are used by the cassette recorder. There is nothing on the tape which guides the heads, or which indicates to you how many tracks exist.

The number of tracks therefore depends on your disk drives. The vast majority of drives for other machines use either 40 or 80 tracks. Forty-track disks use 48 tracks per inch, and 80-track disks use 96 tracks per inch. The Commodore 1541 disk system, however, uses 35 tracks. This does not force you to find any special variety of disks, because the tracks are put in place by the recording head, not by anything on the disk itself.

Once you have accepted the idea of invisible tracks, it's not quite so difficult to accept that each track can also be invisibly divided up.

The reason for this is organisation – the data is divided into blocks, or sectors, each of 256 bytes. A byte is the unit of computer data; it's the amount of memory that is needed for storing one character. Each track of the disk is divided into a number of sectors, and each of these sectors can store 256 bytes. Conventional 40 or 80 track disks use only ten sectors per track, but the Commodore 1541 uses considerably more. On the outer tracks, which are longer, the disk can use 21 sectors, and on the shorter inner tracks it uses 17 sectors. This allows the 1541 disk system to store a lot more bytes per disk than many other disk systems for other computers. The Commodore manual usually refers to 'blocks'; in this book, I prefer to use the name 'sectors' which is used by most other manufacturers.

The next thing that we have to consider is how the sectors are marked out. Once again, this is not a visible marking but a magnetic one. The system is called *soft-sectoring*. Each disk has a small hole punched into it at a distance of about 25 mm (1 inch) from the centre. There is also a hole cut through the disk jacket, so that when the disk is turned it is possible to see right through the hole as it comes round.

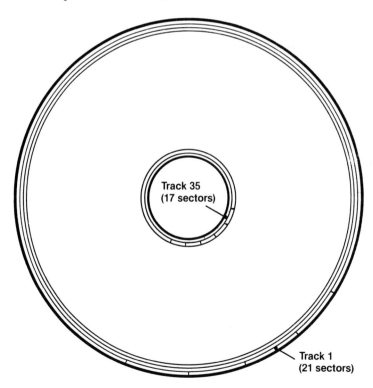

Track 35
(17 sectors)

Track 1
(21 sectors)

Fig. 1.4. How the disk sectors are arranged. These are not visible, because they consist only of magnetic signals.

When the disk is held in the disk drive and spun, this position can be detected using a beam of light. This is the 'marker' and the head can use it as a starting point, putting a signal on to the disk at this position and at seventeen to twenty-one others, equally spaced, so as to form sectors (Fig. 1.4). This sector marking has to be carried out on each track of the disk, which is part of the operation that is called *formatting*.

Formatting disks

Formatting disks, as we have seen, consists partly of the action of 'marking out' the sectors on a disk. The formatting action should also, however, test the disk. This is done by writing a pattern to each sector, and checking that an identical pattern is read back later. Failure to do so indicates a faulty sector, and a disk with such a fault should be thrown away, once you are sure that the fault is genuine. That last remark needs some explanation. When disks are manufactured, they are tested. The best of the bunch can be used for the most demanding recording systems, using double density, both sides of the disk and 80 tracks. If only one side of the disk is good enough, the disk can be sold as single sided. If the disk will not reliably record tightly packed data, it may be good enough to work with single density and with 40 tracks. Never be tempted to try to operate a disk beyond its stated limits, because it has already been tested beyond these limits and has failed! You may sometimes read descriptions (mostly copied from an article in a U.S. magazine in 1978) of how to cut extra holes in a disk jacket and use the other side of the disk. This can work, but it is fraught with problems. One is, as we've seen, that the disk has already been judged as not being up to it. The other is that when you turn the disk round and use its other side, you are revolving the disk the other way, and this inevitably releases some dust that was quite comfortably trapped when the disk was revolving in its original direction. My advice is – don't do it! For your Commodore 1541 disk drive, you can use single-sided, single density disks. At the time of writing, these can be bought for as little as £14.50 for a box of ten if you shop around a bit.

Formatting, then, consists of marking out sectors and testing them. This takes about a minute, but the computer can be used for other things while this is going on, as long as the other things do not call for disks to be used. The reason is that the computer only has to send the formatting command to the disk drive, and the disk drive will then get on with the job of formatting by itself. This leaves the computer free for other jobs. If there is anything wrong with the disk, then the red light on the disk drive will flash to bring the fault to your attention. If you find a disk fault at the formatting stage, then return the disk to the supplier.

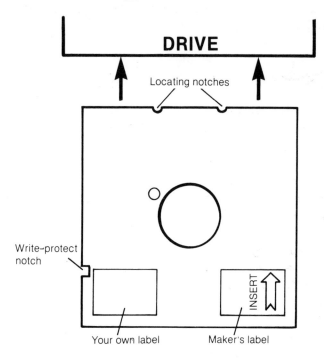

Fig. 1.5. The correct way round for inserting disks.

The formatting action is carried out when two instructions are typed and entered. First of all, insert a new disk in the drive, making sure that it is the correct way round. This is illustrated in Fig. 1.5. The flap on the front of the drive unit is opened by pushing the bar. This allows the flap to lift, and if a disk is already in the drive it will be ejected. Hold your new disk with the label facing up and the notch cutout on your left-hand side. Slide the disk into the slot. Don't use any force to do this, because you can jam the disk if you do so. Press the disk in firmly until it stays put. Now press the bar down until it clicks into place. The disk is now ready for formatting.

You next have to type a command which will allow the computer to take control of the disk drive. This command is:

    OPEN 15,8,15

Then press RETURN. We'll look later at the effect of this and similar commands. Follow this with:

PRINT#15,"NEW0:Name,ID"

and press RETURN. In this last command, there must be no space between the T of PRINT and the hashmark, #. The word NEW can be abbreviated to N, and the 0 (a zero, not the letter O) can be omitted if you have only one disk drive. This zero is the drive number, and when you have only one drive the number is normally 0. You can use a word of up to eighteen letters as the name of the disk, and two characters as the identity code, ID. You will find that the numerals 64 are very often used as an ID by C'64 programmers. If you use more than 18 characters for the name of the disk, the machine will ignore all the characters that follow the sixteenth. The ID characters are placed on each directory entry to identify data that belongs on that disk.

Finally, the formatting action writes on to some sectors on the eighteenth track. This portion is reserved as a way of storing information about the contents of the disk. To put it crudely, the disk system reads the first few sectors of this track to find if a program is stored on the disk, and then to find at which sector the program starts. With this information, the head can then be moved to the start of the program, and loading can start. This part of the track is divided into two regions, known respectively as the BAM and directory. The BAM is the *block availability map*, which keeps a record of what tracks and sectors have been used, and which of them are free for further use. The rest of track 18 is used for directory entries. These are numbers which indicate which track and sector is used for the start of each program or other file that is stored on the disk. Along with this information is the filename of the program (up to sixteen characters) and information that is needed when the file is not a program but some other form of data. When you wipe a program or some data from the disk, all you do is remove its directory entry – the data remains stored on the disk until it is replaced by new data. This can *sometimes* allow you to recover a program that you thought you had erased.

Storage space

How much can you store on a disk? The Commodore 1541 system uses 21 sectors on each of tracks 1 to 17, 19 sectors on tracks 18 to 24,

18 sectors on tracks 25 to 30, and 17 sectors on tracks 31 to 35. This makes a total of 683 sectors. Of these, one set of 19 sectors, the whole of track 18, is used for the BAM and directory entries, and this leaves 664 sectors free for you to use.

Each of these sectors will store 256 bytes, which is a quarter of a kilobyte. Multiply 664 by a quarter, and you end up with a figure of 166K on a single-sided 40 track drive. Not all of this will normally be usable, however, because data is not stored at every point on the disk. Suppose you have a program that is 1027 bytes long. The disk operating system will split this into groups of 256 bytes, because it can record 256 bytes on one sector. When you divide 1027 by 256, you get 4 and a fraction – but the DFS does not deal with fractions of a sector. Five sectors will be used, even though the last sector has only three of its 256 bytes recorded. When the next program is saved it will start at the next sector, so the unused bytes are surrounded and there is no simple way of making use of them. If you save a lot of short programs on the disk, you will find that a lot of space may be wasted in this way. Another way in which space can be wasted if you keep a very large number of very short programs on a disk is that each program will have a separate directory entry, and when the directory track is full no more entries can be accepted. The 1541, however, allows up to 144 directory entries on a disk, so you would have to be very fond of short programs to run out of directory space!

The large amount of storage space, 166K, on a disk contrasts with the 39K or so which you have available for BASIC programs on the C'64. Even this figure can be greatly reduced if you are using a more advanced form of programming language, such as Simons BASIC. For long programs, then, a disk system can be used as a form of extra memory. If a long program is split into sections, the sections can be recorded on a disk and a master program entered into the computer. This master program can then call up different sections from the disk as needed, giving the impression that a very large program is, in fact, operating. The use of a disk system therefore does not only allow you to load programs more quickly and store a lot of data, it also allows you to use the computer as if it had a very much larger amount of memory.

Finally, Fig. 1.6 lists some precautions on the care of disks. These may look rather restrictive, but remember that a disk is precious. It can contain a lot of data, perhaps all of your programs. An accident to one disk, then, can wipe out all your work at the keyboard! Always make a backup copy, and always take good care of your disks. If you leave a fingerprint on a piece of tape you may cause

---

Care of disks

1. Don't bend the disks. They may be called 'floppy disks', but the magnetic coating is liable to be damaged if you bend them.
2. Always buy disks with hub reinforcing rings. The mechanism that clamps the disks in place will soon tear the centres of unreinforced disks. If you have any such disks with programs on them, make back-up copies on to disks with reinforcements.
3. Avoid touching the magnetic surface where the head slot is placed. Never try to take a disk out of its casing.
4. Store your disks, in their envelopes, in a box. You can keep them in the boxes (for ten disks) in which they arrive, or in boxes made for the purpose. Keep them away from dust, smoke, liquids, heat and sunlight.
5. Avoid, at all costs, magnets, or objects that contain magnets. These include electric motors, shavers (not many people shave while they are computing, but you never know), TV receivers, and monitors, telephones, tape erasers, electric typewriters, and a host of other things you might be tempted to place disks on.
6. Don't use a ball point pen to write on to labels on the disk. BEROL make a 'floppy-disk pen' which has a point that will break off if you exert too much force. A felt-tip is suitable, but you must not press hard while writing.
7. Use disks that are suitable for the drive you have. Do not use double-sided disks on a single-sided drive.

Fig. 1.6. Taking care of your disks. They are not as fragile as this might suggest, but each disk can hold a lot of valuable programs.

some loading difficulties on that piece of tape, but it's unlikely that you will lose a whole program. A fingerprint on the surface of a disk could make the directory impossible to read, so that the whole disk would be useless. Similarly, a disk can be demagnetised by strong magnetic fields. You can get these fields around loudspeakers, TV receivers or monitors, headphones, and electric motors. All of these should be regarded as potential disk-killers.

Chapter Two
The Disk Filing System

What does the DFS do?

The disk filing system or DFS is, as we have seen, a program. This program is not written in BASIC, but in the form of direct commands in number code to the microprocessor (the 6502) which operates the Commodore 64. Code of this kind is called *machine code*. (If you want, or need, to know more about machine code, then I suggest that you turn to my book *Introducing Commodore 64 Machine Code*, published by Granada.) The purpose of the DFS is to interpret the disk commands that you type, and convert these into signals that can be used to control the disk system and shift data to and from it.

Note that the name is disk *filing* system, not simply disk system. Filing implies the storage of data (such as string or number arrays) as well as BASIC or machine code programs. The DFS is therefore equipped to carry out the organisation of data which is needed to store it on disk and recover it later. That's something that we'll come back to later in Chapter 5. Meantime, we'll keep to the more straightforward uses of the DFS. Rather than looking at the commands of the DFS in alphabetical order, we'll look at them in the order that is likely to be most helpful to you, starting with the use of disks for storing programs. First, however, we need to look at how the use of a DFS modifies the Commodore 64 machine, and what problems this can create for you.

The first thing that you have to get used to is the order of switching on and off. When the disk system is switched on it needs a short time to prepare for being used, and during this time it's important that it should get no signals from the computer. As you switch on the components of your system, then, you must always ensure that the disk drive is switched on *before* the computer. If you find that you have managed to reverse the order, then switch both off and start again.

You will see on the front of the 1541 disk drive a pair of lights. The one on the left-hand side is green, and it simply indicates that the power is switched on to the drive unit. The red light is a 'busy' warning, and it will be on while the disk unit is operating. You must *never* take a disk out of the drive or put another disk in while this light is on. An error in a disk operation is signalled by this red light flashing, and later in this book we'll deal with how to find what the error is. A few programs as they load will cause the red light to blink irregularly, but you will hear the drive whirring round as well, indicating that this is not an error. When you switch the drive on, you will see the red light come on momentarily. Only when it has gone out can you safely switch on the computer. When you do this, the red light will come on briefly again, then go off. You do *not* have to have any disk in the drive while you switch it on.

Using your memory

Memory is one of the vital statistics of a computer, and it is organised in units that are called *bytes*. Each byte can store one character, but numbers are coded so as to make more efficient use of memory than having one byte allocated for each digit. The total amount of memory that the microprocessor of the machine can cope with in one lump is 65536 bytes. So as to distinguish one byte from another, we number them, starting with 0 and going up to 65535 in our ordinary counting scale. Since 1024 bytes is, in computing language, 1K of memory, the Commodore 64 is described as having 64K of memory ($64 \times 1024 = 65536$). Most modern computers use this amount of memory, but the important quantity is how much of the memory is available for you to use. The C'64 allows you to use almost 38K of the total of 64K. This is about the same as some computers that describe themselves as 48K machines.

An important difference which has been mentioned earlier, however, is that adding a disk system takes no memory from the Commodore 64. One manufacturer sells a 16K computer which has only 7K left when the disk system is added. Adding a disk system to your C'64 leaves you with exactly as much memory as you had before. This is a very great advantage, because it allows you to transfer programs from cassette form to disk form with no risk of running out of memory. The price that you pay for this convenience is that you can only use a Commodore disk drive – the disk drives that you see at such tempting prices in the shops are for any other machines, but not the Commodore!

Loading and saving

We dealt with the formatting of a disk in the previous chapter. Once a disk has been formatted, you can use it for storage. The method that you follow for BASIC programs is very similar to the method that you use for cassette storage. If, for example, you have some BASIC programs on a cassette that you want to save on to a disk, then the procedure is as follows. Connect up the cassette recorder if you have not already done so, and place the cassette that you want to use into the recorder. Place a formatted disk into the disk drive. Load in the program that you want to save. If this program is on cassette, you will have to start by typing LOAD "NAME" (or just LOAD"" if you want the next program on the tape), and pressing RETURN. You will get the familiar message PRESS PLAY ON TAPE, and when you do so the program will start to load. This action of loading from tape should present no problem other than the time it takes. Once the program has loaded, you may want to check it briefly by listing it or running it just to make sure that it is the program which you want. Now type SAVE "MYPROG",8 using whatever filename you have decided to give the program. Remember that the disk system permits up to sixteen-character filenames. You must use a filename when you load or save using disks. When you press RETURN the disk drive will click, and almost immediately (unless it is a very long program) you will see the READY prompt reappear to indicate that the transfer is complete. Shortly after this the red disk drive light will go out, and you will hear the disk motor stop. That's it! The essential difference between this action and the corresponding SAVE action to the cassette recorder is the use of the number 8. This refers to the single disk drive, and if you have one 1541 type of drive, you will always use the number 8 following a disk SAVE command like this. If you have more than one drive, however, you will use 8 for one drive and 9 for the other. Your disk manual advises you on two methods of ensuring that the second drive responds to the number 9.

To load a program that is on disk, you can type LOAD "MYPROG",8 (or whatever filename you have chosen) and press the RETURN key. If the disk is correctly inserted in the drive, it will spin, and the READY prompt will reappear shortly to indicate that the program is loaded and ready. If you used the wrong filename, you will either get the wrong program or an error message, depending on whether a file of the name you used exists. If there is no program called MYPROG on the disk, for example, you will get the error message:

　　　?FILE NOT FOUND　　　ERROR

If, together with your 1541 disk drive, you got a disk which contains six games programs, you will find that they do not load correctly with this command. That's because, like most games programs for the C'64, they are written in machine code rather than in BASIC. A machine code program has to be loaded into the same places in the memory of your computer as it was in the C'64 in which the game was tested. This can be done by adding a comma and then a '1' to the end of the LOAD instruction. For example:

　　　LOAD"DEPTHCHARGE",8,1

will load this game program, and also start it running.

　　Loading is generally much faster than storing, because the DFS carries out a check on data when it records, but not to the same extent when it replays. If you get any sort of error message when you are saving a program, then it's wise to assume that the program has not been saved and to save it again. You can verify that a program has been saved correctly by typing:

　　　VERIFY"name",8

using the same filename as you used to save the program. When you press RETURN, the disk will play back the program and compare it with the version that is still in the memory. This does *not* erase the program in the memory (LOAD would), and allows you a second chance if anything went wrong the first time. As you make more use of your disk system you will find yourself using VERIFY less often. It's useful, however, if you are saving a very valuable program on a disk that is almost full.

　　When you have saved a program on a disk, it's time to take a look at the way the disk keeps track of your program. This is done by reading the directory of the disk. The disk operating system treats the directory as a special file whose filename is $. This filename cannot be used as the filename for a program to be saved on the disk, but you can load the directory into the computer as if it were a BASIC program with line numbers. This is done by typing:

　　　LOAD"$",8

(then RETURN). When the READY message appears again you can inspect this list by typing LIST (then RETURN). You can treat this listing just as if it were a BASIC listing. You can, for example, print it out, and you can even record it under another filename. It's very convenient to keep printouts of your directories. If you have a large number of disks it's also handy to keep a disk which consists of nothing but recordings of directories. You can do this by loading in the directory of a disk, then adding a BASIC line which contains a REM to tell you which disk this is. This can then be saved on to the disk which you use for directories.

```
0   "CBM 1541 VARIETY"  64  2A
28   "1541 BACKUP"         PRG
1    "SOOPER FROOT"        PRG
2    "SOOPER FROOT1"       PRG
57   "SOOPER FROOT2"       PRG
1    "STELLAR WARS"        PRG
2    "STELLAR WARS1"       PRG
52   "STELLAR WARS2"       PRG
1    "DEPTHCHARGE"         PRG
2    "DEPTHCHARGE1"        PRG
57   "DEPTHCHARGE2"        PRG
1    "LABYRINTH"           PRG
2    "LABYRINTH1"          PRG
63   "LABYRINTH2"          PRG
1    "THE QUEST"           PRG
2    "THE QUEST1"          PRG
79   "THE QUEST2"          PRG
1    "PATIENCE"            PRG
2    "PATIENCE1"           PRG
27   "PATIENCE2"           PRG
281 BLOCKS FREE.
```

Fig. 2.1. A typical directory for a disk.

If you have only one drive that's all you need, but with two or more drives you will have to select the drive number in the command by using LOAD"$",8, or LOAD"$",9, etc. When you press RETURN, the disk will spin briefly and display the information that is illustrated in Fig. 2.1. This shows on the top line the drive number, the title of the disk (if any), the ID characters, and the characters 2A. The 2A is a version number which appears in current type 1541 drives. Following the heading, you have a line of entry for each program or other file. Each line shows the number of sectors (blocks) that the file uses, the name of the file, and the type of file. When you first start to make use of disks you don't need much of this, but you will probably find it more useful later. At first, the most useful feature of the catalogue is the fact that the program filenames are shown. The disk system shows these files in order of storage on the disk. Since the disk is used by filling the inside tracks first, the order of files in the catalogue is the order of files on the disk starting at the centre track, track 17.

Sometimes, when you try to save a program, you will find that the disk system will not accept the save. This is almost always because a program with the same filename has already been saved on that disk. The 1541 disk drive will not replace one program with another of the same name *unless you specially want it to*. This is a very useful protection for your programs, because it is not always convenient to keep a note of the directory. Remember that when you load the directory it will *replace* any BASIC program in the memory. If you have just completed a program and you want to save it, then don't load the directory to find if you have used a filename already! This will mean losing your program, which wasn't exactly what you intended.

If you really want to replace a program, however, this can be done by a small addition to the SAVE command. Suppose, for example, that you have a program on the disk which is called "INDEX". You have just developed version 2 of this program, but you want only one version on the disk. You can type:

SAVE"@:INDEX"

and press RETURN. The @ has the effect of deleting the existing program on the disk and substituting your new version. Make sure that you have a backup, just in case. I have seen an absent-minded C'64 user replace a good program by a copy of the directory in this way! It's always a good idea to list your program first before you use this command. If you have more than one disk drive, incidentally, the drive number can be placed between the @ and the :.

Disk commands

Because the disk system for the C'64 contains its own computing circuits, complete with memory, a lot of the actions that we use to control the disk system have to be carried out by sending command words to the disk system itself. The words SAVE and LOAD are

C'64 command words, which operate on the cassette system if you forget to add the 8 after the filename. There is another set of commands, however, which applies to the disk system only, and which has to be sent to the disk drive. This is done by using a special 'hotline', a channel for commands only, which is identified by a number, 15. This channel is opened by the command:

OPEN15,8,15

and after this has been done you can send commands by using a PRINT#15, – followed by the command that you want to use. (We noticed this action in use in Chapter 1, in connection with formatting a disk.) The commands which can be sent in this way can all be abbreviated, and it's more convenient to do this as it avoids some typing. As we meet each command word we'll look at the full version, and then at the abbreviation.

Retitling and erasing

As your use of disks increases you may find that you want to group files that are related in some way on to one disk. It is then very helpful if you can give this disk a title which will remind you of what it contains. You might, for example, have a disk full of utility programs of various types, and a logical title would be UTILITIES. You can use a title name of up to eighteen characters. Normally you would title a disk at the time when you formatted it, but quite frequently you may want to erase and retitle without reformatting. Reformatting is a lengthy process, whereas retitling is fast. Retitling, however, *wipes out the directory*, so it's not something that you would do to a disk that already held a number of stored programs. The retitling command is:

OPEN 15,8,15
PRINT#15,"NEW0:newname"

Notice that the only difference between this command and the reformatting command is that this version does not use an ID number following the disk name. This is why the command is faster. When a disk is reformatted the ID code is placed on each sector. When the disk is erased and renamed only the directory track is changed. Appendix A deals with a method for retitling a disk without losing the stored programs. We'll look at the way of renaming a program in the next chapter.

One very important command that you should get used to at this stage is "Initialise". Sometimes, when you are developing a program that uses disks, things will go haywire and the program will stop with an error message and the red light glowing on the disk drive. Even worse, you may find that the disk keeps spinning and the keyboard does not have any effect until you press STOP and RESTORE at the same time. After any 'crash' of this kind, you should send a command which restores the disk to normal if any commands have been left half-done. This is achieved by using:

PRINT#15,"I"

or, if channel 15 has not been opened, just with:

OPEN15,8,15,"I"

This will spin the disk, sort it out, and then stop the disk with the red light extinguished. You should always do this before you get to work on the program to find out why it has stopped.

The error system

When you have a BASIC program, or a direct command, which has a fault in it, the machine will stop and bring the fault to your attention. This is done by means of an error message on the screen, and you can then change the program or the command and try again. There are, as you might expect, disk system errors which can also be reported, but the method is not quite so straightforward and obvious. If you mistype a *computer* command (like LOAD or SAVE), perhaps by omitting the first quotemark or by incorrect spelling of the command word, then the command will never get to the disk system. It will be caught by the operating system of the computer and you will get the usual SYNTAX ERROR message. If, however, you get an impossible command to the disk system, you don't always get an error message directly.

When you ask the disk system to find a program name which doesn't exist, then the action is just as it would be when you have an error in a BASIC program. In this example, the disk system looks for the filename in its directory, doesn't find it, and the screen shows the message:

?FILE NOT FOUND   ERROR

When you use only straightforward LOAD and SAVE commands, then you will get the necessary messages like this.

You often need to issue other commands to the disk system, however, as we have seen. These make use of the special *command channel*, a sort of hotline to the disk system which is used for issuing other types of commands. The NEW command is just one of these, all of which make use of the PRINT#15 command to get the message to the disk system. Now when an error occurs because of one of these commands, you get *no screen message*. All that there is to warn you that something has gone wrong is that the red light on the front of the disk drive will be blinking *after* the drive has stopped spinning. This light is a warning that an error has ocurred in the disk drive but has not been delivered to the computer. It does *not* cause the disk system to stop operating, and you can send another command if you like. What it can mean, however, is that some action that you wanted to carry out has not been carried out. You may, for example, think that you have saved some data on to the disk – but you have not!

Sometimes the light may blink even when an error message appears on the screen. For example, if you place an unformatted disk or a disk that has been recorded by a different type of computer in the drive, you may get both types of error reports. Trying to read the directory of a disk that has been recorded on another type of computer will really puzzle the system. On the screen you will see the ?FILE NOT FOUND   ERROR message, but the drive light will be blinking too. The reason is that there is more to tell. The screen shows FILE NOT FOUND because, as far as the computer is concerned, that's what has happened. The disk drive has not delivered the goods and this is the appropriate message. The disk drive, however, has its own error message system, and the message that it has to deliver is:

74   DRIVE NOT READY   00

Now if we forget about the numbers for the moment, the message DRIVE NOT READY is a much more revealing one than FILE NOT FOUND. It draws your attention to something really wrong with the drive or the disk, and since this is the usual message for an unformatted disk, it should lead you to check the disk.

The snag, however, is that these disk system messages do not get delivered automatically to you, just as the directory of the disk is not read automatically. To read the disk error messages you have to get them delivered over the 'hotline' to the computer and printed on the screen. Unfortunately, it's not possible to do this with direct

```
10 OPEN15,8,15
20 INPUT#15,A$,B$,C$,D$
30 PRINT A$,B$,C$,D$
```

Fig. 2.2. A short program to read error messages. Use this as a subroutine in your disk programs.

commands, and you need a short program. This program is noted in your 1541 disk manual, and also in Fig. 2.2. The program opens the hotline to the disk drive, inputs four string values from this channel, and then prints them. Once this has run, the error light stops blinking because when the error report has been read the drive no longer stores the error. The first string holds the error number, the second holds the error message, and the third and fourth hold the track and sector number if the error is caused by a fault in the disk itself. (The last two numbers are zero unless something is wrong with the disk.)

This is not exactly an ideal way of finding out disk errors, and it is much less convenient than the systems that other computers use. We have to make the best of it, however. The snag about it is that a short BASIC program is needed. It is possible to write the instructions in machine code so that they can be held in a protected piece of memory and run by a SYS command. A much easier method, however, is to incorporate the three lines of the BASIC error-reading program into any program that uses disks, so that the reading of errors is automatic while you are using that program. This is not so useful when you are not working with a program. Every now and again you may be retitling files or carrying out other actions on your disks, with no program loaded. When you get an error message you *may* know why the light is blinking, but it would be good to know exactly.

This is simple enough if you have typed the error program or loaded it from a disk. Typing RUN (then RETURN) will run the error program, and show you what has gone wrong. The snag is that you will quite often want to load in the directory. Each time you load in the directory, the operating system will wipe out your error program. What you need is some way of being able to use the error program, but also to load in anything else that is of interest without zapping the error program. This can be done with a bit of 'poking'.

The C'64 stores a BASIC program in the form of a set of number codes in the memory of the computer. Each memory location has an identity number, its 'address'. Now the first address that is used by BASIC is stored in the form of two numbers so that the machine can find this address quickly. These numbers are stored in addresses 43 and 44, and for our purposes address 44 is the important one. The number that you will find here (by the command PRINT PEEK(44)) is 8. Now when we type or load in the error-reading program it will be stored at a set of addresses in the memory, for which this number 8 is a key. If you change this number to a higher value, then the C'64 can't find the error program – to all intents and purposes the error program does not exist.

Try this now. Type or load in your error program, and LIST it. Now type:

POKE 44,9   (press RETURN)

and LIST again. This time, there is no listing. The program seems to have disappeared. Now type:

POKE 44,8   (press RETURN)

this time, and LIST. Behold, the program is listed! What we have done is to shift the address at which the computer looks for a BASIC program.

You can therefore make use of your error program in this way. Type it or load it in when you start work. Then use POKE 44,9. Now as you work on your disks, carrying out the actions that we shall be looking at in the following chapters, you may get error messages. When this happens, type POKE 44,8 (RETURN) and then RUN. The error program will print up the error message, the red light will stop blinking, and you can then use POKE 44,9 to get back to your work. When you want to load in the disk directory, *always* make sure that you have used POKE 44,9 first. The directory loads as if it were a BASIC program, and it will replace any other program at the same addresses. If you have used POKE 44,9, you can load and list the directory and then, by using POKE 44,8, you can still make use of the error program even after loading the directory. This minor piece of organisation can make working with disks less of a hassle than it would otherwise be.

This simple way of protecting your error program is only intended for use along with the directory. If you want to load in another BASIC program and run it, then typing POKE 44,9 is not enough, because the program will not RUN. (For details of this point you can consult my book *Introducing Commodore 64 Machine Code*.) If, incidentally, you have a much longer program in the computer and you want to protect it when you look at the directory, then type:

PRINT PEEK(46)

Note whatever number this gives, and then POKE 44, with a number which is one larger. If the PEEK gives 14, for example, then POKE 44,15 to protect your program. You can then load the directory, look at it, and POKE 44,8 to return to your program. You have to LIST each time to see what is stored at the different addresses.

Chapter Three
Digging Deeper

Hexadecimal codes

Unless you program in machine code, you probably haven't encountered the *hexadecimal scale*. If you only use your disk system as a convenient way of storing programs and data, and you have no intention of trying to read data from damaged disks or to write machine code disk routines or copy disks which are copy-protected, then you can skip what follows and reserve it for later. At some stage, however, you will probably want to make use of this information, and this is as good a place for it as any other.

'Hexadecimal' means scale of sixteen, and it's a way of writing numbers that is much better suited to the way that the computer uses number codes. Our ordinary number scale is *denary*, scale of ten. This means that we count numbers up to nine, and the next higher number is shown as two digits, 10, meaning one ten and no units. Similarly, 123 means one hundred, two tens and three units. This counting scale, invented by the Arabs, replaced the Roman numbering system many centuries ago (except, oddly enough, for writing the copyright dates of films and TV programs!). A denary number for a byte may be one figure (like 4) or two (like 17) or three (like 143). Hexadecimal (usually shortened to 'hex') is a much more convenient code for these numbers, and for address numbers. All one-byte numbers can be represented by just two hex digits, and any address by four hex digits.

One hex digit, then, can represent a number which, written in ordinary denary, would be between 0 and 15. Since we don't have symbols for digits higher than 9, we use the letters A,B,C,D,E and F to supplement the digits 0 to 9 in the hex scale, as Fig. 3.1 illustrates. The advantage of using hex is that we can see much better how address numbers are related. For example, consider the address for the start of BASIC in the ROM of the C'64. This is the address which

Denary	Hex		Denary	Hex
1	Ø1		9	Ø9
2	Ø2		1Ø	ØA
3	Ø3		11	ØB
4	Ø4		12	ØC
5	Ø5		13	ØD
6	Ø6		14	ØE
7	Ø7		15	ØF
8	Ø8		16	1Ø

Fig. 3.1. How the numbers 0 to 15 are written in hex.

is used when you type RUN and press RETURN. In hex this is A000, whereas in ordinary denary numbers it is 40960. The C'64 makes a lot of use of what are called 'page 0 addresses'. These are addresses which *in hex* start with the digits 00. They cover the range 0000 to 00FF in hex. In denary these numbers are 0 to 255, and it's not exactly easy to understand, unless you know the hex equivalent, why they should be called 'Page 0'! Let's take a formal look, then, at what this scale is about.

The hex scale

The hexadecimal scale consists of sixteen digits, starting with 0 and going up in the usual way to 9. The next figure is not 10, however, because this would mean one sixteen and no units; and since we aren't provided with symbols for digits beyond 9 we use the letters A to F. The number that we write as 10 (ten) in denary is written as 0A in hex, eleven as 0B, twelve as 0C, and so on up to fifteen, which is 0F. The zero doesn't have to be written, but programmers get into the habit of writing a data byte with two digits and an address with four even if fewer digits are needed. The number that follows 0F is 10, sixteen in denary, and the scale then repeats to 1F, thirty-one, which is followed by 20. The maximum size of byte, 255 in denary, is FF in hex. The maximum size of address in the memory of the computer, 65535, is hex FFFF. This is the number that we refer to as 64K. The 'K' means 1025 in denary, $400 in hex.

When we write hex numbers, it's usual to mark them in some way so that they aren't confused with denary numbers. There's not much chance of confusing a number like 3E with a denary number, but a number like 26 might be hex or denary. The convention that is followed by users of the Commodore 64 is to mark a hex number with the dollar sign ($) placed before the number. For example, the number $47 means hex 47, but plain 47 would mean denary forty-seven. The machine itself will *not* recognise the use of $ to mark a hex number and cannot convert it to denary, so that you cannot enter numbers like $2B or $028A. If you are using some types of utility programs that recover data from damaged disks, or which alter the machine operating system, you may have to enter numbers in hex. These utility programs usually contain routines for the conversion of numbers between hex and denary scales, so that you never need to carry out hex arithmetic for yourself. The program called DISPLAY T & S which is at the back of your 1541 manual contains these routines, and it displays its information in hex.

Backing up

One feature of a disk storage system which is less pleasant is that an accident to a disk can result in the loss of a lot of information. If you break a cassette tape, it's possible to splice the tape and, with some juggling, lose only a part of one program. If you damage a disk, it's likely that all of the information on the disk will be lost as far as conventional LOAD commands are concerned. This does not mean that the information cannot be recovered from the disk; but this is a desperate measure, not to be undertaken lightly. It makes sense, then, if you have a disk full of valuable programs or data, to make a backup copy as soon as possible.

One sensible measure is to make a second copy of each program as you put it on disk. If you have bought programs on disk, however, you will need to make a backup copy – or two copies if the disk is a valuable one. Unfortunately, the disk system of the C764 does not have a backup command. You can copy individual files, but not the whole of a disk.For many purposes, however, copying a file is enough because you may only have one valuable program or data file on the disk. Unfortunately, the operating system of the 1541 disk drive does not allow you to copy a file from one disk to another. To do so, you will have to load the file into memory from one disk and save it to another. This is straightforward enough when the files are BASIC programs, but the task is a lot more difficult when the files are machine code programs or data files. Fortunately, utility programs are available for carrying out this essential task. We'll look at a very useful backup utility later.

Backing up is easy when you have twin drives. With two drives, you can use a utility program to cause everything on the disk in drive 0 to be copied to the disk in drive 1. The process is accompanied by a lot of clicking and whirring, as one disk is read and the other written, but at least you don't have to attend to the process. You can make yourself a cup of coffee while it is all happening. An alternative, if you still have your cassette recorder, is to keep backup copies on cassettes. It's much safer, however, to backup on to another disk, and to keep this backup disk in a cool, safe place well away from all the hazards to disks, such as loudspeakers, TV receivers, electric motors and anything else that uses magnets of any kind. Later in this book we'll take a look at the sort of utility programs that are available for the C'64.

Copying a named file

Very often, you don't need to backup a complete disk, just make a copy of one file that is on a disk. For some curious reason, the operating system of the 1541 does not contain any command which can be used to copy a file from one disk to another one. It does, however, allow you to make another copy of a file *on the same disk* but using another name. This is not quite so silly as it sounds, because if you update a file regularly you will probably want to keep the older version around just in case you need it. Since you can't have two files bearing the same filename, it's convenient to change the name of one file before you record the next one. You might, for example, use the name "NEWONE" for the up-to-date version, and "OLDONE" for the old one. The command which makes this copy-and-name-change operation possible is COPY, which can be abbreviated to C. This has to be used in a syntax which is not quite so simple and straightforward as the previous examples.

You must start by typing:

OPEN 15,8,15 (press RETURN)

which prepares the disk drive for a command. You then type:

PRINT#15,"COPY:NEWONE=:OLDONE" (press RETURN)

and you will hear the drive spin into action. The result of the action will be to create a file called NEWONE which contains all the information that is also in the file OLDONE. These 'files', remember, can be anything that is recorded on the disk, whether BASIC programs, machine code programs or data. If your drive is not drive 0, then you will have to place the drive number just before the colon. No drive number is needed if you are using just one drive, drive 0.

It's possible, however, that a file with the same filename of NEWONE may already exist on the disk. If this is so, the copy action will not proceed and you will see the red light blinking on the front of the disk drive. If you then read the error report from the disk, you will get the FILE EXISTS message on the screen. This is a reminder that you are in danger of wiping out a file which you may have forgotten about. If you actually want to do this – as for example, when you are updating a file, and want to keep using the same name – you will have to delete or rename the old file before you use COPY. We'll deal with both of these processes later in this chapter.

Deleting files

As well as copying and creating files on to disks, you may want to delete files. You may, for example, have developed a BASIC program through several versions, and wish now to delete all the old versions. You may, to take another example, have an accounts program which creates a file of inputs and outputs of money, and which needs to read a data file in and write one out to update the data. This also *may* require you to delete an old file – we'll discuss data filing in more detail in Chapter 5. Whatever your need, deleting a single file is carried out using the SCRATCH command. This is yet another command that has to be sent over the 'hotline' to the disk drive, and the syntax is:

    OPEN 15,8,15   (press RETURN)

followed by:

    PRINT#15, "SCRATCH:PROGNAME"

A drive number can be included ahead of the colon, and the name of the program will be whatever name appears in the directory for that program. Even if you pick a name that does not exist the drive will go through the motions of deleting the name and there will be no *error* message. There will always, however, be a message *in the error system*. If you scratch a file (real or imaginary!) and then run the error-reporting program of Chapter 2, you will find a report such as:

01   FILES SCRATCHED   00

waiting for you. This is *not* an error, so the error light does not blink. The first number in the report is the number of files that have been deleted by the command. This is necessary because it's possible to delete more than one file by this action – we'll look at that point later.

   This SCRATCH action, which can be abbreviated to S, does *not* remove the data of the file from the disk. What it does is to remove the catalogue entry, so that the space on the disk can be made use of by a later entry. This will happen only if the new file is shorter than the deleted file, or of the same length. If this is not the case the new file will use another part of the disk, and the space that was used by the deleted file will remain unused until we do something about it. It is possible to recover the contents of a deleted file by writing a new catalogue entry, but this comes into the realms of advanced programming and is definitely not the sort of thing you want to attempt while you are getting to know your way round the DFS! The SCRATCH action will not work on a disk that is 'write-protected' – see later in this chapter.

Wildcards and wiping

So far, we have always worked with a single named file on each command. You can, however, amend the commands slighly so that more than one file can be affected, or so that you have to specify less information. The amendment involves the use of 'wildcards' in the filename. A wildcard means a character that can take the place of a letter or a group of letters in a filename. The two wildcard characters are * and ?. Of these, the ? sign can be used as a substitute for any single letter, and the * can replace any group of letters. Suppose, for example, that you typed:

   LOAD"*",8   (press RETURN)

just as you might type LOAD"" when you were using the cassette system. What you actually load depends on what you have previously done. If you have just switched on and put a disk in, the action will be to load the first program that is on the disk. If you have been using other programs, then the LOAD"*",8 action will reload the last disk program that you used. If you have changed disks, you may get a FILE NOT FOUND error message, however. This is usually caused by an ID mismatch. The previous program that you used may have had an ID of 64, and all of the programs on this other disk have an ID of IS, for example. The red drive light blinks after this effort, and if you use your error message program you will see the full report, such as:

    29   DISK ID MISMATCH   17
    05

You will see other numbers following the MISMATCH word. These numbers are, respectively, the track and sector numbers of where the fault was found. It's information that you don't need at the moment, but this is a good time to be introduced to what it is about.

The use of LOAD"*",8 is not particularly useful feature, and it can quite often load in a program that you did not expect, unless you keep a very close track of what you are doing! Where the * sign becomes useful is to replace several letters in a filename. Suppose, for example, that you have a program which is called 1541 BACKUP. You may very well have such a program, because at the time of writing it was being supplied with the 1541 drives. Instead of tediously typing out the name of this program each time that you want to load it, you can type simply:

    LOAD "1*",8   (press RETURN)

This will load *any* program whose filename starts with a '1'. If, as is likely, only one program answers that description, this will be the one that is loaded. If you have two programs which start with a '1', then the rules are as for using LOAD"*",8 – you will get the one you used last, or you will get whichever comes first in the directory. What it amounts to is that you will get the first program which starts with a '1' that the head of the disk drive comes across when the disk spins. You might call this CBM Roulette.

Another useful feature of this 'wildcard' character is that you can load selected parts of a directory. If you have a disk which contains a large number of programs, perhaps the maximum number of 144, it can be very tedious looking through them all. You can obtain utility programs (see *Commodore Computing International*, August 1983, page 56) which will sort your directory into alphabetical order. A simpler option is to ask for a limited directory. Suppose, for example, that you want only the program names that start with N. By typing:

LOAD"$:N*",8   (press RETURN)

you can load in just the directory entries which start with the letter 'N'. You will still get the directory header which shows the name of the disk and its ID characters, but the list of programs will be shorter. (Note that the manual uses the drive number 0 in this command. I found that this was not necessary on my drive.)

We have earlier looked at the use of SCRATCH as a way of deleting one single named file on a disk. You can make use of wildcard characters to remove more than one file. Suppose, for example, that you wanted to remove all the files that started with the letter T. This would be done by:

OPEN15,8,15
PRINT#15,"SCRATCH0:T*"

because of the presence of the wildcard character * in the title. A less drastic deletion might be of every file that starts with A, has three letters, and which ends in D. For this, you would use the single-character wildcard, the ? mark. By typing:

OPEN15,8,15
PRINT#15,"SCRATCH0:A?D"

you will remove all files of this specification, including AND, ASD, ARD, but leaving ANY, ADF, BED and any others that do not match the specification exactly.

A more drastic way of wiping a disk, if you want to remove *all* of the files, is simply to format it again. Remember, however, that reformatting takes a lot of time, and it's much better simply to use NEW to clear the directory and rename the disk, as we dealt with in the previous chapter. If you use the SCRATCH command to remove files selectively, you will be left with a disk which bears a strong resemblance to a piece of Emmental cheese: full of holes, unwanted bytes of data that are not used by any file that is in the current catalogue. We can make more efficient use of the disk by reallocating this space, so that all the files we actually have in the directory are put into the first parts of the disk, rather than scattered all over it. This requires the use of VALIDATE.

Every now and again, you will get a DISK FULL message on a disk which you know should have plenty of space on it. This is because files have been deleted from the disk but subsequently-entered files have been too large to fill the gaps. The gaps therefore remain, preventing the addition of data. The disk *is* full, but not of wanted data! VALIDATE reallocates space on a disk by the simple method of reading files from the disk and writing them on again, using all the disk space in the lower-numbered sectors. The syntax follows a pattern which should be fairly familiar to you by now. You type:

    OPEN 15,8,15   (press RETURN)
    PRINT#15,"VALIDATE"

You can abbreviate VALIDATE to V, if you like. Using this command will cause a fair amount of activity from the disk as it checks and rechecks the block availability map and shuffles the data around. Wait until the disk has stopped spinning before you load the directory to see the result.

Protecting disks and programs

Just as we have a number of methods of deleting files from disks, we also have a number of methods of preventing this from happening. One method is universal to all disk systems on all machines. It makes use of the 'write-protect' tab on the disk. If you hold a disk as you would if you were inserting it into the 1541 drive, you will see a small rectangular slot cut from the left-hand side of the jacket. This is the 'write-protect notch'. When the disk is in the drive the presence of this notch is detected, either mechanically or by a light beam. If the notch is unobstructed, the disk can be read and written. If the notch is covered, then the disk can only be read, not written again. In each pack of disks you will find a set of small sticky tabs that can be used to cover this notch to make a complete disk 'write-protected'. If you want to re-use such a disk, you only have to remove the tab. Remember that another protection also exists for programs and for serial files (see later for an explanation of serial files). The protection is simply that you can't replace a program by one of the same name unless you use the '@:' ahead of the filename.

Renaming files

Occasionally we want to give a new name to a file. We could, of course, load the file, save it under another name, and then delete the old filename. This is not necessary because all that has to be changed is the catalogue entry on the disk. This can be done using the

RENAME command. Renaming is particularly important for data files. Suppose, for example, you have a program which creates an index of names and numbers, and which saves its index to disk under the filename INDX. If this program has been used before there will be a file called INDX on the disk and the disk system will refuse to create another file of the same name.

There are three ways out. One is to delete the existing INDX file and, if necessary, make space by using VALIDATE on the disk. Another way is to add the '@:' ahead of the filename so as to force the disk system to replace the old file by the new one. The third way is to rename the offending file. This last approach is rather better, because it preserves the old file and the new one now finds another place on the disk. RENAME has to be followed by the drive number, the new filename, an equals sign, and then the old filename, in that order. Renaming will not occur if the disk is write-protected. Taking an example, suppose that you have a program which is called TEST and you want to rename it TRUE. The procedure is to type:

OPEN 15,8,15   (press RETURN)
PRINT#15,"R:TRUE=TEST"(press RETURN)

and the renaming operation will be carried out. As usual, you can put a drive number ahead of the colon if you are using more than one drive or if your single drive is not drive 0.

Chapter Four
Disk Utilities and How To Use Them

Disk utilities are programs which are designed to allow you to use your disk drive to better purpose. In this chapter I shall deal with the disk utility programs which are listed in the 1541 manual, and with the '1541 BACKUP' program (by Michael Schaff) which is currently being given away (with six machine code games on the same disk) with the 1541 disk drives. We can also take a very brief look at what we might expect from a utility disk.

A utility disk, as the name suggests, is a disk on which are stored several routines, mostly in machine code, which should be of use to disk users. A disk of this type may be advertised under various names. Whatever the title, the aims are always to supplement the facilities that are available in the DFS. These are features which allow us to recover information from a damaged disk, and also to read ASCII codes from disks that were made on other machines. The most valuable feature, then, for a utility disk is a disk sector reader and editor. At the time of writing, no utility disk was available for the C'64, but at least two were being written. If such a disk might be of interest to you, then I suggest you contact Mick Bignall at Microport, 7 Clydesdale Close, Borehamwood, Herts WD6 2SD, or alternatively Simple Software Ltd., 15 Havelock Road, Brighton, Sussex BN1 6GL. By the time that this book appears, both of these sources should have utility disks available. In the meantime, we can look at what can be done, with what we have at present.

The disk sector editor

The purpose of a disk sector editor is to allow you to see what bytes are stored in any sector of a disk, and to modify these bytes if necessary. Simply viewing the bytes is not harmful, but careless changing of bytes can make a disk almost unreadable, so some caution has to be exercised. If you are likely to want to make use of a disk sector editor, it pays to experiment first with a spare copy of a disk. *Never* work with a sector editor on any disk for which you have no backup of any kind, unless you are absolutely certain that you will only be reading sectors, not changing them. Some disk editors intentionally make it difficult for you to alter bytes. Others make it all too easy!

To avoid being too general and therefore too vague, I shall describe the facilities that are available at the moment, using just the routines that are printed in the 1541 disk manual or which are being given away with the drives at present. From that, I shall tell you what to expect from a utility disk when one is available. Since the principles of utility disks are broadly similar, a detailed description of one will serve as an outline for all.

I'll start with the program that was enclosed with my disk drive, but which was not documented in any way. This is a pity, because it provides the essential purpose of allowing the backup of any 1541 disk, a provision that is lacking in the operating system. The program is by Michael Schaff, and can probably be bought separately if you did not get it with your disk drive. The program title is 'SINGLE DISK BACKUP V1.0', and it is written in BASIC, not in machine code. When the program runs, the screen clears and you are presented with a set of boxes which will be used to present information and messages. These boxes are headed, in order from top to bottom, BACKUP COMMAND, BUFFER, DISK, DISK STATUS, EXECUTING, and OPERATOR INTERVENTION. The OPERATOR INTERVENTION box is used to contain messages to you, to tell you when you have to insert disks.

The purpose of the program is to make a complete backup of a disk, so that it will *always* start by formatting a new disk. You must be careful that you do not accidentally wipe out the contents of a valuable disk when you use this program, because formatting will always remove anything that was previously recorded on a disk. Formatting will not be possible, however, if the disk has a write-protect tab fitted. When the program starts, a cursor flashes in the top box that is headed BACKUP COMMAND. Your answer is expected to be B or D. If you use B, then you get what is called 'BAM backup'. This means that only each program that is entered in the directory will be transferred to the new (desination) disk. If you select D, then the whole contents of the disk will be transferred, irrespective of what is in the directory. This takes much longer, but probably allows a lot of 'copy-protected' disks to be backed up. Even if you have only one program on the disk, then, using D will cause the whole contents to be copied. This is clearly a waste of time, so you should always use the B option unless you know that there is information on the disk that you need but which is not noted in the directory. When you select B or D, and press RETURN, the cursor then moves to the DISK box and the word DESTINATION is printed. This is a prompt for you to enter the name and the ID letters of the new disk. If you simply press RETURN, the name that will be used is CBM 1541 BACKUP, and the ID will be 64.

When this has been done, the OPERATOR INTERVENTION box is used to signal to you to place the destination disk in the drive. This is where you must be careful. If you place the disk that you want to backup into the drive at this point, you may wipe it clean and be left with nothing to backup. It pays, then, to label your disks very clearly before you start this backup operation. If you want to be quite certain, then put a tab around the write-protect notch on your source disk. When you insert the destination disk into the drive and press RETURN, the disk is formatted and the name and ID characters are written to the disk.

Assuming that all is well, and the DISK STATUS box shows the message:

00, OK,00,00

then you are prompted to place the source disk, the one that you want to copy into the drive. When you do this and press RETURN, you will get a message in the EXECUTING box to the effect that the program is reading the BAM (block availability map) from the source disk. You will see the title and ID of this disk printed, and you are then asked to VERIFY SOURCE DISK FOR BACKUP. If you press any key that is not N, the backup will proceed. Pressing N allows you to insert another source disk and repeat the read of the BAM. If you use as a source disk one which carries the same ID as your destination disk, you will get an error message to the effect that the ID numbers are not unique. This is because disks may have to be swopped several times in the course of a backup, and using different IDs prevents you from getting the disks mixed up from this point on.

If you opt to carry on with the backup, then you press a key that is not N and you will get a message in the EXECUTING box. This will be READING DATA INTO BUFFER, and as the disk spins you will see a bar growing in size in the box which is marked BUFFER. This indicates that the memory of the C'64 is being filled with data from the source disk. If you are using the D option, this buffer will have to be filled and emptied several times. If you are using the B option, and are copying a disk with only a few programs on it, the buffer may need only one fill operation. When the buffer is full, or the disk completely read, you are prompted to put the destination disk into the drive. When you have done so, and pressed RETURN, the buffer starts to empty. The machine is copying the contents of its memory that were filled from the source disk into the destination disk. As this proceeds, you will see the visual indication in the BUFFER box. If the first load of data did not complete the backup, you will be prompted to place the source disk into the drive again, and so on. This will continue until all of the programs that were recorded on the source disk have been transferred to the destination disk.

Because the program is in BASIC it is rather slow, but it carries out its job satisfactorily. One advantage of being in BASIC is that you can interrupt the program between reading the source and writing to the destination. If you know what you are doing, you can then alter some of the bytes of data in the buffer. This is a way of making programs 'invisible', so that their names do not appear in the directory. I must stress, though, that unless you have had a lot of experience with machine code this is not something that you should try on any disk that you value! Always experiment with spare copies.

The manual utilities

The 1541 manual contains some utility programs, of which the listings at the back of the book (Appendix C) work and are useful. Since no guide is given on how to use them, however, they are not quite so useful to you until you know more about them. This looks as good a place as any to deal with these programs, which are called DIR, VIEW BAM, DISPLAY T & S, CHECK DISK and PERFORMANCE TEST. Of these, DIR and DISPLAY T & S are the most immediately useful.

The DIR program allows you a menu of four options. By typing D (no need to use RETURN) you will get the directory of the disk, avoiding the need to perform the LOAD"$",8 routine when you want to look at several directories. There is no option to print the directory on the CBM (or other) printer, which is a pity. You could, however, add such a routine. The DISPLAY T & S program contains printer routines which you can adapt for the DIR program. The S option displays the disk status by reading the command hotline for errors. The most useful command letter is '>', which allows any command to be passed to the disk system. If, for example, you want to validate a disk, you select the '>' option, type V and press RETURN. There is no need to OPEN or PRINT, since these operations are carried out by the program. You don't need to use quotes around the command either. Any command that is normally sent by using a PRINT#15 can be sent to the disk in this way. DIR is therefore a very useful little routine for operating on your disks.

The DISPLAY T & S program allows you to read what is stored at any part of the disk. The bytes are shown in hex, so that you will have to brush up (or learn) your hex codes in order to make effective use of this. When the programs runs, you are asked whether you want to use screen or printer to display the results. Normally, you will want to use the screen option at first until you are quite certain which part of the disk is of most interest to you. Having answered this, you press RETURN and the disk spins briefly. You are then asked which track and sector you want to view. If you type 0,0 (press RETURN) in reply, the program will end. If you type sensible numbers, then the display (assuming that you have picked the screen option) will start. This scrolls onwards unless you stop it with the RUN/STOP key. If you use the RUN/STOP key to halt the list, then you can continue by typing CONT (press RETURN). You should not abandon the program after pressing RUN/STOP, because this can cause problems with the disk system. Instead you should wait until you have a chance to answer the TRACK,SECTOR question with a 0,0.

The program will print out 128 bytes ($7F in hex) before you get the message CONTINUE(Y/N). At this point you can stop the listing or allow it to continue. If you opt for continuing, the bytes will be listed until all the 256 bytes of a sector have been shown on the screen. At this point you get a message which informs you of the next track and sector numbers, and you can opt to continue or stop. If you stop at this point, you get the original TRACK,SECTOR message, and you can leave the program in an orderly way by entering 0,0 as the track, sector numbers. While the program is running, any bytes which correspond to ASCII code values are displayed as characters. This means that you can recognise features such as disk names, ID codes and filenames, and also text that is part of a program. This makes it reasonably easy to identify directory entries and files on the disk, and to note their positions by track, sector and byte numbers. Remember, however, that the numbers that this program displays are *all in hex*.

Editing a disk

The other utilities are more straightforward, because there are no options to be taken. None of them, however, allows you to make repairs on a disk which might have a damaged directory entry. This is the action which a fully-fledged disk editor program allows, and which can be so useful.

Different utility programs have different ideas of what is meant by editing a disk. Some programs take this to mean that each byte can be read and a decision made whether to leave it or change it. Another interpretation is that the editor simply prints on the screen the bytes in each sector of the disk, with no provision for change.

In general, though, you will be looking through a sector for some specific purpose. This will usually be to check a catalogue entry or to check that data is correct. The most important feature of the catalogue sectors is the information on where data is stored. Take, for example, the data that is shown in Fig. 4.1 for a program file. This is the first file on the disk, and its catalogue is on track 18, sector 1 – remember that the sectors are numbered from 0, not from 1. In this example, the first two bytes of the sector are 00 and FF, which are used to indicate the end of this directory. The third byte is 82, which is a 'type of file' indicator. The digit that follows the 8 is used to indicate the type of file, and will be 0 if the file has been deleted. For a program, the digit is 2. The next two numbers, 11 and 00, are for the track and sector of the first part of the program. Remember that these are hex numbers, so this means track 17, sector 0. This, then, is where you can expect to find your program stored. The program name in ASCII codes then follows, and then a set of A0 characters. In the second line, the only important portion for a BASIC program is the last couple of numbers. These, in this example, are 1C and 00. If you arrange them in reverse order, as 001C, this is the number of sectors that the program uses, in hex. In this case, the number 001C corresponds to 28 sectors. This is the number that is also shown in the directory printout at the left-hand side of the program name when you use LOAD"$",8 and LIST.

When you create other types of files more of the directory entry will be used, but for a program file these are the only parts of the directory entry that are relevant. A disk editor program would allow you to change these entries. One very important possibility is to merge BASIC programs. Many programmers like to keep a set of standard subroutines which are used in all of their programs. If each subroutine is held on a disk, then a disk utility can be used to add a

```
00 :12 04 82 11 00 42 41 43 4B 55 50 A0 A0 A0 A0 A0 :  FGH BACKUP
10 :A0 A0 A0 A0 00 00 00 00 00 00 00 00 00 00 1C 00 :
20 :00 00 82 11 01 50 4C 49 4E 47 45 A0 A0 A0 A0 A0 :  FGH PLINGE
30 :A0 A0 A0 A0 00 00 00 00 00 00 00 00 00 00 01 00 :
40 :00 00 82 11 03 44 49 52 A0 A0 A0 A0 A0 A0 A0 A0 :  FGH DIR
50 :A0 A0 A0 A0 00 00 00 00 00 00 00 00 00 00 04 00 :
60 :00 00 82 11 05 52 45 41 44 45 52 52 4F 52 A0 A0 :  FGH READERROR
70 :A0 A0 A0 A0 00 00 00 00 00 00 00 00 00 00 01 00 :
80 :00 00 82 11 06 4E 45 57 46 49 4C 45 A0 A0 A0 A0 :  FGH NEWFILE
90 :A0 A0 A0 A0 00 00 00 00 00 00 00 00 00 00 04 00 :
A0 :00 00 82 11 02 54 52 41 43 4B 53 45 43 54 4F 52 :  FGH TRACKSECTOR
B0 :A0 A0 A0 A0 00 00 00 00 00 00 00 00 00 00 08 00 :
C0 :00 00 82 13 00 48 45 41 44 45 52 A0 A0 A0 A0 A0 :  FGH HEADER
D0 :A0 A0 A0 A0 00 00 00 00 00 00 00 00 00 00 01 00 :
E0 :00 00 82 14 02 50 53 41 56 45 4C 4F 41 44 A0 A0 :  FGH PSAVELOAD
F0 :A0 A0 A0 A0 00 00 00 00 00 00 00 00 00 00 01 00 :
```

Fig. 4.1. The catalogue data which is contained on track 18, sector 1.

subroutine to a program which is in the memory. You cannot do this by using the LOAD command, because LOAD automatically wipes out the program which was previously in the memory. Many games programmers, in fact, write their programs on other machines, and then transfer the codes into the C'64 to get over these difficulties. Another action that can be contemplated is changing the identity number of a file. If, for example, you had a BASIC program saved, its number would be $82 (130 in denary). Changing this to $81 (129) makes the disk system treat this as a serial file, not as a BASIC program, so that it cannot be loaded by the LOAD command! When a good disk editor is available, life will be made much easier for dedicated disk-users!

Machine code and other bytes

The ordinary operating system of the C'64 does not provide for the saving of machine code. Machine code programmers, however, will generally use assembler programs, such as the excellent MIKRO cartridge, to write code, and these assemblers contain routines for saving code. If you write machine code by poking numbers into memory, then the code can be saved like a BASIC program by shifting the addresses for the start and end of BASIC. This method is detailed in my book *Introducing Commodore 64 Machine Code*. An attractive alternative is to save machine code as a serial file, by peeking each byte in a loop program and saving it on disk. The following chapter contains details of serial files.

Text files

A text file means a set of ASCII codes stored on the disk or in the memory of the computer. A BASIC program is *not* an ASCII file, because the reserved words of BASIC are each coded as a number between 128 and 255. These codes are called 'tokens', and a file that consists of text only, such as a file that has been created by a word processor, will not contain such tokens. Text files have to be recorded so that they can be replayed into the memory of the computer with no gaps, and word processor programs contain their own routines for controlling the disk drive. Unless you are writing your own word processor program, then, this is not something that you have to worry about.

Chapter Five
BASIC Filing Techniques

What is a file?

I have used the word 'file' many times in the course of this book to mean a collection of information which we can record on a disk. Programs in BASIC are one type of file, and the only type, incidentally, which permits the use of LOAD and SAVE in a straightforward way. In this chapter I shall use the word 'file' in a narrower sense, to mean a collection of data that is separate from a program. For example, if you have a program that deals with your household accounts, you would need a file of items and money amounts. This file is the result of the action of the program, and it preserves these amounts for the next time that you use the program. Taking another example, suppose that you devised a program which was intended to keep a note of your collection of vintage 78 r.p.m. recordings. The program would require you to enter lots of information about these recordings. This information is a file, and at some stage in the program you would have to record this file. Why? Because when you load a BASIC program and RUN it, it starts from scratch. All the information that you fed into it the last time you used it has gone – unless you recorded that information separately. This is the topic that we're dealing with in this chapter, recording the information that a program uses. The shorter word is *filing* the information.

Knowing the names

You can't discuss filing without coming across some words which are always used in connection with filing. The most important of these words are *record* and *field*. A record is a set of facts about one item in the file. For example, if you have a file about vintage steam locomotives, one of your records might be used for each locomotive type. Within that record you might have wheel formation, designer's name, firebox area, working steam pressure, tractive force. ... and anything else that's relevant. Each of these items is a field, an item of the group that makes up a record. Your record might, for example, be the SCOTT class 4–4–0 locomotives. Every different bit of information about the SCOTT class is a field, the whole set of fields is a record, and the SCOTT class is just one record in a file that will include the Gresley Pacifics, the 4–6–0 general purposes locos, and so on. Take another example, the file BRITISH MOTOR-BIKES. In this file, B.S.A. is one record, A.J.S. is another, Norton is another. In each record, you will have fields. These might be capacity, number of cylinders, bore and stroke, suspension, top speed, acceleration ... and whatever else you want to take note of. Filing is fun – if you like arranging things in the right order.

Disk filing

In this book, because we are dealing with the C'64 disk system, we'll ignore filing methods that are based on DATA lines in a BASIC program, or on the use of cassettes. Though you may be experienced in the use of filing with cassette systems, I'll explain filing from scratch in this chapter. This is because many buyers of the C'64 machine nowadays start from scratch with a disk system, and have never used cassettes. If it's all familiar to you, please bear with me until I come to something that you haven't met before.

To start with, there are three types of files that we can use with a disk system: serial files, relative files and random access files. The differences are simple, but important ones. A *serial* (or *sequential*) *file* places all the information on a disk in the order in which the information is received, just as it would be placed on a cassette. If you want to get at one item, you have to read all of the items from the beginning of the file into the computer, and then select. There is no way in which you can command the system to read just one record or one field. More important, you can't change any part of a record, or add more records to such a file. A *relative file* is a kind that applies only to the Commodore disk system. A relative file is stored like a serial file, but each entry into the file causes a kind of directory entry (though not in the directory track of the disk). This allows any part of the file to be found much more quickly than would be possible if the file were just an ordinary serial type. In addition, it allows records to be replaced and more records to be added. A *random access file* does what its name suggests – it allows you to get from the disk one selected record or field without reading every other one from the start of the file.

You might imagine that, faced with this choice, no one would want to use anything but random access files. It's not so simple as that, though, because the convenience of random access filing has to be paid for by a lot more complication, as we'll see in Appendix A. For one thing, because random access filing allows you to write data at any part of the disk, it would be very easy to wipe out valuable data, or even the directory, with a program that was badly designed. We'll start, then, by looking at serial files, which are also easy to record on cassette. All of the DFS commands for serial filing are very similar to the commands of the cassette filing system. This makes the change very easy if you have been using filing on cassette and you then upgrade to disk. If you have never used cassette files, of course, it's all new.

Serial filing on disk

We'll start by supposing that we have a file to record, called CAMERAS. On this file we have records (such as Nikon, Pentax, Canon, Yashica and so on). For each record we have fields like film size, shutter speed range, aperature range (standard lens), manual or automatic, and so on. How do we write these records? First of all, we need to arrange the program that has created the records so that it can output them in some order. The usual order will be to take the records in a chosen order, and output the fields of the record in an order as well. Figure 5.1, for example, shows how we might arrange this part of a BASIC program so as to output a number of records, with five fields to each record. The number of fields is five, so the fields are put out using a FOR N=1 TO 5 loop. The number of records isn't fixed, so we use a GOTO loop which keeps putting out records until it finds one called "X", which is the terminator. Note that we haven't used an array for holding these items, because an array has to be dimensioned and we don't know in advance how many items we will have. The appearance of "X" is tested twice. Strictly speaking, this isn't necessary, but it can avoid the problems that you meet when you have to GOTO to form a loop.

That deals with the organisation of the data for putting on to disk, but how do we actually put it on the disk? There are several stages,

```
100 DIM FD(5):X%=0
110 PRINTCHR$(147):PRINT"TYPE X TO END
ENTRY"
120 INPUT"RECORD NAME ";RC$:X%=X%+1:IF
RC$="X"THEN 190
130 REM NEED TO RECORD THIS!
140 FOR N=1 TO 5
150 PRINT"FIELD ITEM ";N;" ";:INPUT FD$
(N)
160 REM NEED TO RECORD THIS ALSO!
170 NEXT
180 IF RC$<>"X"THEN 120
190 X%=X%-1:REM LAST RECORD IS BLANK
200 PRINT"THERE ARE ";X%;" RECORDS ON T
HE FILE"
```

Fig. 5.1. How to organise data for disk writing. The example uses five fields in a record.

and the first one is to allocate a *channel number*. This is a type of code that the machine will use to distinguish files. The C'64 machine can deal with several sets of serial files at one time, five to be precise. It's most unlikely that you will ever want to use more than two serial files at a time (probably one for reading and one for writing, for example), but it's better to be generous than to be stingy. Each time you want to make use of a file, then, you must have a channel number (or 'handle') allocated. You have to do this for yourself by allocating a channel number, using numbers between 2 and 14 inclusive. The C'64 reserves channel numbers 0 and 1 for its own purposes, and channel 15 is reserved as a hotline to the disk operating system. You can take your pick of what's left. In the course of the rest of this book, I'll use various different numbers simply for the sake of variety. I tend to avoid the numbers 3 and 4 simply because they are used so much in the printer commands. Avoiding their use for disk numbers helps avoid confusion.

The purpose of this channel number is to organise data. The disk stores all data in units of 256 bytes (actually a few bytes less, but that's a detail at present). It wouldn't make sense to spin the disk and find a place on the disk just to record one byte at a time, so when you record or read a disk it's always one complete sector at a time. Some of the memory of the C'64 has to be used to hold data which is being gathered up for recording or which is being replayed. The channel number is an identifying number for the piece of memory that is being used, so that the machine finds the correct data in the correct part of the memory. Using channel numbers like this avoids the need for you to allocate parts of the memory for buffers.

Opening the file

After that short diversion, back to our filing·program. Before we start to gather the data together for filing, we need to 'open a channel' for the data. This is done using the OPEN command. OPEN has to be followed by three numbers when it is used for files in this way. The first number is a file number. This can be any number between 1 and 255, but it makes life a lot easier if you make this number the same as your channel number. I have never come across a need to use a file number that was not equal to the channel number, and you probably won't either. In addition, if you make the numbers identical you won't have trouble ·when you start using commands that require the channel number in place of the file number. Remember the old motto: Simplicate and add lightness!

The next number is the number for the disk operating system, the familiar 8. The last number is the channel number. If, for example, we use:

OPEN 2,8,2

then we will have opened file 2, channel 2 to the disk system. We can then either send information to the disk or take it from the disk. That's not all we need for serial filing, however. We also need to specify the name of the file, its type, and the direction of data flow. The name can, like any other filename, be up to 16 characters. The type, if you are using a serial file will be S. The direction will be R if you are reading, or W if you are writing. The complete OPEN statement, then, might look as follows:

OPEN 2,8,2":AIRCRAFT,S,W"

to write a file called AIRCRAFT. As always, you can place the drive number ahead of the colon. When you read the directory of the disk the file name will be shown along with the typename of SEQ (sequential), so that you know that you can't read the file using LOAD. If we open another file for reading it will be allocated another channel number, so that we can keep the files separate. To avoid confusing yourself, though, try to keep as few files on the go as possible!

The use of the OPEN command opens a file – which means that

we can make use of that file. It also means that the disk is prepared for the file. Any file that exists on the disk already and has the same name of AIRCRAFT will prevent you from opening this file, however. To get round that problem you can modify the name of the file so that it will automatically delete any file of the same name. This is done in the usual way by adding the @ mark just ahead of the colon in the title. You can also place a drive number ahead of the colon, but if you have only one drive there's not much point. In addition to recording the filename, sectors will be reserved for the file.

Printing to the file

It's at this stage that we need to make use of the loops in the writing program. Within these loops we need to have a line something like:

3000 PRINT#2,FD$(N)

PRINT#2 means put the information out on channel 2. This, because of our previous OPEN statement, leads to the disk system, so that PRINT#2 will eventually put out to the disk system the data that follows. In this example, it's FD$(N). N is the number in the FOR...NEXT loop, so that as the loop goes round we will put on to the disk field(1), then field(2), then field(3)... and so on. We also need to write the *record* name, and this is done within the loop by using a line such as:

130 PRINT#2,RC$

without using an array (because of the unknown amount of dimensioning).

Figure 5.2 shows an example of a very short and simple program of this type which has been adapted from the first example. You can enter anything you like into this, but it makes more sense to enter something that you can easily check. Since the file is called aircraft, you could make each record name the name of an aircraft type, and each field some feature of the aircraft, like wingspan, engine details, number of crew, and so on. You can, of course, easily change this program so that it has another title that suits the information that you might want to use.

Before we move on, consider what this has done. It has created a file called Aircraft, and allocated a channel number of 2 to this file. It has then stored the data as it came along, in the sequence of

```
10 OPEN2,8,2,":AIRCRAFT,S,W"
100 DIM FD(5):X%=0
110 PRINTCHR$(147):PRINT"TYPE X TO END
ENTRY"
120 INPUT"RECORD NAME ";RC$:X%=X%+1:IF
RC$="X"THEN 190
130 PRINT#2,RC$
140 FOR N=1 TO 5
150 PRINT"FIELD ITEM ";N;" ";:INPUT FD$
(N)
160 PRINT#2,FD$(N)
170 NEXT
180 IF RC$<>"X"THEN 120
190 X%=X%-1:REM LAST RECORD IS BLANK
200 PRINT"THERE ARE ";X%;" RECORDS ON T
HE FILE"
210 CLOSE2
```

Fig. 5.2. A program which writes to a serial file.

RECORD, then FIELDS. Finally, the file has been recorded and closed by using CLOSE2. This last step is very important. For one thing, you don't actually record on the disk any of the information in this short program until the CLOSE2 statement is executed. That's because it would be a very time-consuming business to record each item of a file one at a time. What the DFS does, remember, is to gather the data together in memory. This is a 'buffer' piece of memory, and it will be written to the disk only in one of two possible circumstances. One is that the buffer is full, so that there is one sector full of data (256 bytes) to write. The other is that there is a CLOSE2 type of statement in the program. For a large amount of data, the disk will spin and write data each time the buffer is full. The CLOSE# command then writes the last piece of data, the one which doesn't fill the buffer. It also writes a special code number, called the *end-of-file code* (EOF). This can be used when the file is read, as we'll see later. If you forget the CLOSE statement you'll leave the buffer unwritten, with no EOF – and cause a lot of problems in your programs. Forgetting the CLOSE is called 'leaving your files open', and you wouldn't like to be caught like that, would you? The biggest danger is when you are testing a program. If there is an error, such as a syntax error, which stops the program from running, there will be no CLOSE2 carried out and the files will be open. If you had typed a lot of data, you would lose it if you then went on to correct the program and run it again. The correct procedure is to close all of the open channels. In this example it's easy – you only have to type CLOSE2 and press RETURN. This ensures that your data will be recorded. When you use an INPUT statement to gather up the data, you can find that with a lot of data you will hear the disk start and stop at intervals. That's an indication of the buffer transferring data to the disk. You can't use the keyboard while the transfer is taking place, but the time that's needed to write a sector is fairly short.

Getting your own back

Having created a file on disk, we need to prove that it has actually happened by reading the file back. A program which reads a file must contain, early on, a command which opens the file for reading. This is another OPEN, and it makes sense to use another channel and file number, just in case you want to carry out both reading and writing in quick succession. The file number and channel number can be the same, or you can use different numbers, but the *name* of the file *must* be the same. If we recorded a file using the name AIRCRAFT, then we must not expect to be able to read it if we use CAMERAS – or any other name. Misspelling can bedevil you here! Once the channel number has been allocated we can read data with INPUT, which will be followed by the file number. This reads an item from the disk, and will allocate it to a variable name or print the item, according to what we have programmed. The number of reads can be controlled by a FOR...NEXT loop if the number is known, or it can make use of the EOF marker if the number is unknown. The operating system of the C'64 uses a variable ST which changes from 0 when an end of file is found. By testing for ST changing value, then, we can make the program stop reading the file at the correct place.

The example of Fig. 5.3 shows both methods in use. The number of fields has been five, so that a FOR...NEXT loop can be used to control the input of the fields. The number of records, however, has not been settled by a FOR...NEXT loop, so we have to keep reading the file until the EOF byte is found. This is done in line 120 by testing ST. If ST is not zero, then the file is closed and the program ends. Note that the disk does *not* spin each time you press a key to get another record. This is because a complete sector is read each time, and if the information that you want is all on the same sector the disk need not be used. Sorry if I seem to be labouring this point, but a newcomer to disks sometimes finds it difficult to remember.

```
100 DIM FX(5)
110 OPEN 3,8,3,":AIRCRAFT,S,R"
120 PRINTCHR$(147):INPUT#3,NM$:IF ST<>0
THEN 240
130 PRINT"TYPE IS ";NM$
140 FOR N=1 TO 5
150 INPUT#3,FX$(N):NEXT
160 PRINT"WINGSPAN ";FX$(1)
170 PRINT"LENGTH ";FX$(2)
180 PRINT"CREW NO. ";FX$(3)
190 PRINT"ENGINES ";FX$(4)
200 PRINT"RANGE ";FX$(5)
210 PRINT"PRESS SPACEBAR TO CONTINUE"
220 GET A$:IF A$=""THEN 220
230 GOTO120
240 CLOSE3:PRINT"END":END
```

Fig. 5.3. A program which reads the serial file.

Now this simple example shows a lot about serial filing that you need to know. When you use disks, then the name that is used with OPEN is the file name for the file on the disk. Any other file that is later recorded with the same name will not overwrite this file, so the system provides for good file security. This is an important point to emphasise if you have been using cassettes, because you have more control over a cassette. You can write a file called INDEX at the start of the tape, for example, then wind the tape on slightly and record another, different, file with the same name. You certainly can't record two files with identical names on one disk. In addition, a file is closed by writing the EOF character. How, then, can you update a file, particularly if you want to add more items to the end of the file?

Updating the file

There are two answers, if we stick to serial filing. One possibility, which is the simplest one for short files, is to load the whole file into the memory of the computer, make the alterations (your BASIC program will have to be written so as to provide for this), and then write the file again, wiping out the earlier version. The other possibility is to open two files, one for reading and the other for writing. You don't need to have dual disk drives for this, though it makes life much simpler if you do. This means that the computer will maintain two buffers. You read one record from the reading file and you can, if you want, display it. If it's all right, it's then written (to the buffer initially). If the record has to be modified, you can do this. If extra records have to be added, that is equally simple. Each time a buffer empties the disk will spin and a read or write will take place. This 'simultaneous' operation is possible because of the use of different channel numbers which control different buffers. In practice, it's a matter of writing your program to suit. Figure 5.4

```
100 DIM FX(5):X%=0
110 OPEN 4,8,4,":AIRCRAFT,S,R":OPEN 5,8
,5,":MORE,S,W"
120 PRINTCHR$(147):INPUT#4,NM$:IF ST<>0
THEN 160
125 PRINT#5,NM$
140 FOR N=1 TO 5
150 INPUT#4,FX$(N)
155 PRINT#5,FX$(N):NEXT:GOTO120
160 INPUT"AIRCRAFT NAME ";NM$:X%=X%+1:I
F NM$="X"THEN 230
170 PRINT#5,NM$
180 FOR N=1 TO 5
190 PRINT"FIELD ITEM ";N;" IS ";:INPUT
FD$(N)
200 PRINT#5,FD$(N)
210 NEXT
220 GOTO160
230 X%=X%-1
240 PRINT"YOU HAVE ADDED ";X%;" ITEMS"
250 CLOSE4:CLOSE5:OPEN15,8,15
260 PRINT#15,"S0:AIRCRAFT"
270 PRINT#15,"C0:AIRCRAFT=0:MORE"
280 PRINT#15,"S0:MORE"
290 CLOSE15
300 PRINT"END":END
```

Fig. 5.4. Extending a serial file by reading, rewriting and renaming.

shows a simple program which allows you to extend the file that was created by the program of Fig. 5.3. Note, however, that the files use different names because I have assumed that both files will be on the same disk. We must therefore end the program by deleting the old file and changing the name of the newly-created file (the extended or changed file) so that it has the same name as the old file. This can be done from BASIC by using the S(SCRATCH) and C(COPY) commands just as we would use them direct from the keyboard. One point we have to be *very* careful about, however, is closing files. The S and C commands have to use channel 15, and this has to be opened. These commands, however, *will not work if the other Channels are open*. This is only briefly mentioned in the manual. In this program, no provision has been made for altering any of the records that are read from the old file. This is a routine which you could easily add for yourself by putting a GOSUB in at new lines 121 and 151.

Relative files

Serial files are very useful for a lot of purposes, but not if you want to be able to obtain a record out of a very large number. With a long program in the memory of the C'64, there would not be much memory left to store a great number of records at a time. This means that you would have to read your records in as an array, test each one to find if it was the one you wanted, and then read another lot in if you couldn't find the one that you wanted. This could take a long time, and it would be much more satisfactory if you could pinpoint the record that you wanted and just read that one (and possibly some others) from the disk. This implies random access, and random access filing can be achieved with the 1541 disk system, as Appendix A demonstrates. Random access filing is by no means easy, however, and for the type of data filing that normally needs to use random access the 1541 drive offers a different method. It is called relative filing and it has a lot of the advantages of random filing with few of the disadvantages. We'll spend the rest of this chapter, then, looking at relative files and how to use them. In the next chapter, I'll give an example of a much longer program which makes use of relative files to achieve a random access database. In other words, this will be a program that allows you to file facts on the disk and get them back whenever you want them.

File facts

A relative file has to be made up from a number of records, like any other file. In each record, however, each field must have a fixed maximum length. The length of a field is the number of characters that can be stored, plus one. The reason for the 'plus 1' is that when you enter a field into the computer you press the RETURN key, and this puts a 'carriage return' character at the end of the field. You have to choose for yourself how many characters will be needed in each field. You might, for example, feel that a field of 15 characters would be enough to store any field that contained the name of a country. You would then have to make sure that no name that you entered contained more than 15 characters (by taking LEFT$(MN$,15), for example). This might mean that a country name like Papua New Guinea would be chopped to Papua New Guine, but this would still be enough to recognise the country by. When you have settled on a length number for a field in your record, every one of these fields must be of that length. It doesn't matter if a name doesn't fill a field because the computer will *automatically* fill up the field to the number of characters that you have chosen, using blanks which don't appear when the name is printed. When you have several fields in each record, as you normally do, then you don't have to use the same number of characters per field. It's convenient, as you will see, if you can, but it saves a lot of space on the disk if you keep each field to the most useful size. For telephone numbers or post codes, for example, it would be foolish to use fields of 15 characters.

The most important feature of relative filing is that the disk operating system keeps a track of the files for you. This is done by setting up a set of 'side sectors', which are a form of directories to your file. The machine will then search through these side sectors for the record that you request, get the track and sector number from this data, and load the sector that contains the record that you want. All of this could be done in other ways, but only with a lot of hard programming work.

Relative rules

On any computer there is always a price to be paid for convenience, and in this case the price is that you have to construct your filing program according to a set of rules. We have seen that you need to fix the number of fields per record and the number of characters per field. You have to use a special form of OPEN command for the file, and you must ensure that there will be at least one blank character between each pair of fields when the file is recorded. One important point is that a relative file is not protected in the way that programs or serial files are protected. If you have a file called "MYDATA" opened and with 20 items recorded, then it is possible to replace these 20 items with a different 20, to alter one of the 20, or to add more items. Your program, then, must be constructed so that you will not accidentally zap out a file of data. There is nothing in the disk operating system that would prevent you from doing this.

It's time now to look at some details. Any relative file will require two channels to be opened. One of these will be the command channel, number 15. The other can, as usual, be any number between 2 and 14, but because of the usc of 3 and 4 for other purposes it's always best to use 5 to 14. The relative file is created *whenever the correct OPEN instruction is used*. The name of the file must start with a colon (:) or, if you have more than one drive, with the drive number and colon, such as '0:'. You have to follow this with a comma, the letter L and then another comma. All of this is enclosed by quotes. You then have to add a number. The reason for this is that each record will consist of fields, and each field will have a length (number of characters). Since these numbers are fixed, each record will consist of the same number of characters on the disk – even if a lot of these are blanks. You must add one character to allow for the carriage return and another to allow for a space between fields, so that the size of the record is:

Sum of field sizes+2×(number of fields)

This number *must not exceed 255* and is added in the form:

+CHR$(number)

to the OPEN command. CHR$ will operate correctly only on a number less than 256, which is why you have to be careful about the size of the record. An example of a correct OPEN statement for a relative file would then be:

OPEN6,8,6,":MYDATA,L,"+CHR$(150)

which would create a file called MYDATA, each record of which had a length of 150 characters. It's because of this fixed length feature that the disk system can find each record so easily.

It looks reasonably straightforward, but there's one slight problem. Because of the way that the disk operating system works, attempting to write data to a file like this will cause an error message! The message is RECORD NOT PRESENT, error number 50, and it appears because the OPEN command for a relative file can be for reading or writing. When you open the file for the first time and write to it, nothing has yet been recorded on the file so the error message is technically correct – there *is* no record present. You don't want to let this error message stop the program, however, so you must arrange to test the error channel (number 15) each time you write to the file. If the error is number 50, the RECORD NOT PRESENT error, you then ignore it and carry on. If there is any other error, though, you will have to print the error and stop. All of this can be done by calling a suitable subroutine.

Since this is not a serial file, we have to pass some more information to the disk operating system. We must, in particular, pass details of the record number. If the record number is 1, then the disk will write the record on the first available piece of track. If the number is 20, the disk will have to count out 19 records (which is 19 times the number of characters per record) to find space. The point about this is that you can write record number 1, and then record number 20, without having written numbers 2 to 19 between them. When you do write these other records, there is space left for them. This is another important difference between relative files and serial (sequential) files.

The information on the record has to be passed along the command channel, number 15. It uses a PRINT#15, command, and this must be followed by "P", meaning 'pointer'. Following the "P", you arrange four numbers, all in CHR$( ) form. The first number is the channel number for the relative file. The second and third numbers are the coded form of the record number. The last number is the position within the record. This allows you to read individual fields of a record, not just the whole record, if you want. A typical example of this command is:

PRINT#15,"P"CHR$(5)CHR$(1)CHR$(0)CHR$(1)

This would prepare for a read or write on channel 5, using the first record and starting at the first character in the record. Before we get to grips with a sample program, however, you need to know how to code the record number. The number is coded as two digits. Each of these must not exceed 255, and the lower one must come first. If you wanted to use 8, for example, it is coded as CHR$(8)CHRS(0), and 255 would be coded as CHR$(255)CHR$(0). When the record number is more then 255, though, you have to use the other CHR$ number as well. This is because no single CHR$ number must be allowed to exceed 255. You can find what is needed by dividing the record number by 256. The whole number part of this is the number that is used *second*. The difference between the record number and 256×(second number) is used as the first number. In case that looks too much like algebra, take an example. Suppose we want to code the record number of 885. Now, 885/256=3 and a fraction. Never mind the fraction, because the 3 is the important bit. This is the *second* number in the coded form. Now work out 885 − (256×3), which gives you 117. This is the number that you use in the first CHR$ position. The final coded form, then, is:

CHR$(117)CHR$(3)

You don't have to go working out these numbers for yourself, though, because a subroutine will take care of them for you. What you *do* need to remember, however, is that the record number must not exceed 65535. This is because the maximum size of number in each CHR$ is 255, and if you use CHR$(255)CHR$(255) as your coding, then this corresponds to the number 255*256+255, which is 65535. That's a lot of records!

Data writing

Figure 5.5 shows a program which will obtain name and address data from you, and write it on the disk. There is a program printed in

```
10  OPEN15,8,15:GOSUB500
20  OPEN6,8,6,":DATA,L,"+CHR$(110)
30  GOSUB1000:N=1
50  PRINTCHR$(147):RESTORE:NT=1
60  FORJ=1TO5
70  READTX$:PRINTTX$,:INPUT NM$:GOSUB150
0:IF LEFT$(NM$,1)="X"THEN 100
80  PRINT#15,"P"CHR$(6)CHR$(L)CHR$(H)CHR
$(NT):GOSUB1000
90  PRINT#6,NM$:GOSUB1000:NT=NT+22:NEXT:
N=N+1:GOSUB1100:GOTO50
100 CLOSE6:CLOSE15:PRINT"END":END
400 DATANAME,ADDRESS1,ADDRESS2,ADDRESS3
,ADDRESS4
500 PRINTTAB(13)"INSTRUCTIONS"
510 PRINT:PRINTTAB(1)"YOU CAN USE THE P
ROGRAM TO ENTER NAMES"
520 PRINT" AND ADDRESSES INTO A FILE CA
LLED"
530 PRINT" -'DATA'. IF YOU DO NOT CHANG
E THE
540 PRINT" VALUE OF 'N', THIS FILE WILL
 REPLACE"
```

```
550 PRINT" ANY PREVIOUS FILE OF THAT NA
ME."
560 PRINT:PRINT"  PRESS SPACEBAR TO PRO
CEED."
800 GETA$:IF A$=""THEN800
900 RETURN
1000 INPUT#15,A,B$,C,D:IF A<20THEN RETU
RN
1010 IF A<>50THENPRINTA,B$,C,D:STOP:RET
URN
1020 RETURN
1100 L=N:IF L>255THEN H=INT(L/256):L=L-
256*H
1110 RETURN
1500 NM$=LEFT$(NM$,20):RETURN
```

Fig. 5.5. Using a relative file for writing.

the manual for this purpose, but it is more complicated and there are misprints. I'll go over this example in detail, so that you can see why each step is carried out. It's very important to do this for these filing actions, because you can spend a lot of time just staring at error messages unless you have an example to follow.

The program starts by opening the command channel and calling a subroutine which prints instructions on the screen. Line 20 then opens channel 6, which is the channel that will be used for relative filing. The name that will be used for the file is DATA, and the record length will be 110 characters. Line 30 then calls the error routine to check that all is well with the disk system. The position in the record is represented by the variable N, and this starts with a value of 1. The subroutine in line 1100 then converts the number N into two characters, H and L, which can be used in the CHR$ statement when the pointer has to be positioned. In line 50 the screen is cleared and the DATA list restored, and the record number NT is also set to 1. This ensures that you start a file from record number 1. If you wanted to use this routine to write any numbered record you would need a subroutine which allowed you to input a number here.

A loop starts in line 60. The planning of this program has allowed for five fields in each record, so each field has to be entered and recorded. In line 70 the name of the field is read from the DATA line, and this name is printed. We are using, for the sake of simplicity, twenty characters per field, and when you type the data (NM$), the subroutine at line 1500 chops each entry to this size if it is larger.

Line 80 is important. This is the command to the disk system which places the 'pointer', and will ensure that the whole record goes in the correct place. The "P" ensures that the pointer is positioned, and the CHR$(6) ensures that this refers to channel 6. By using CHR$(L) and CHR$(H), we let the numbers that have been produced by the subroutine in line 1100 postion the record pointer. The position within the record is then set by the variable NT, which starts with the value of 1. As usual, the error channel is checked by the GOSUB1000. Line 90 then prints the value of NM$ into the correct position in the buffer. It doesn't go to the disk, remember, until enough has been gathered. The disk is checked for errors, and the NT=NT+22 advances the position of the pointer in the same record. We have to use 22, because the number of characters is 20 and we have to add one for the carriage return and one for a space. The loop then repeats, so that each field is input and written to the buffer in the correct field position. The record number, N, is then incremented, converted to H,L form, and the program repeats from line 50. The entry is stopped by entering as a name anything that begins with X. You could choose 0 or any other character that you liked to terminate entry.

When entry is terminated, line 100 closes the channels, prints the word END and ends the program. That's the sequence of events in this writing program, and we now only need to look at the subroutine. At line 500, we have brief instructions. These are, as always, accompanied by a 'PRESS SPACEBAR' message, and then line 800 is executed. This allows you as much time as you need to read the instructions before you get to the serious work. It also allows you to change disks if you want to keep the data on another disk. The subroutine at line 1000 reads the error report along channel 15. The error number is assigned to variable A, and if this is less than 20 we want to ignore the error. (In this version of the Commodore disk system, an error number which is less than 20 *can* be reported but is meaningless.) Line 1010 tests for error 50. This is the RECORD NOT PRESENT error, and if any other error is present line 2020 will print a full report, and stop. The RETURN that follows STOP allows you to continue with CONT after sorting out the problem. If the error number was 50, then line 1020 is run, and this simply causes a return, with no error message. If you want to see why, just insert PRINT B$ in this line before the RETURN! Line 1100 deals with converting record numbers into H,L form, and 1500, as we saw earlier, prevents you from using a name that is longer than 20 characters.

Now each time that you use this program it will create a file called

DATA, and it will start from scratch. This may not be what you want, and you can provide for adding to the file very easily. If you know, for example, that you already have the file DATA created, with 40 entries, then if you make N=41 in line 30 you can continue adding to the file. The only change that this needs to the program is a subroutine. This should ask "DO YOU WANT TO EXTEND THE FILE" and, if you do, ask for the record number. This is assigned to N, followed by a GOSUB1100, and then you return to line 50. There are no safeguards here to ensure that you don't start at the wrong place, but that's a matter of how you want to construct your program.

Reading back

Having created a relative file, we now have to look at the problem of reading it back. Once you have been through the process of writing, reading looks a lot simpler. For one thing, the file now exists on the disk, and opening the file to read it is a simpler operation. You need only OPEN,8,6,"DATA" this time, because the disk system will have a note that DATA is a relative file. Figure 5.6 illustrates the processes for reading the file. Line 200 opens the channels, and line 220 asks you for a record number. This is assigned to variable N as before, and broken into two parts, H and L, in the subroutine. The screen is cleared, the DATA list is restored, and the position in the record, variable NT, is set to 1. The loop which gets five fields then starts in line 250. The title is read from the DATA list, and then line 270 finds the correct position in the buffer as before. Line 280 then reads the first field item. If, incidentally, you do *not* have the file DATA on the disk, you will get the error message NO CHANNEL. This is not what you might expect, and it can be very frustrating until you realise what it really means. The title and the field item are then printed, and the loop continues to read in all of the fields.

In general, the routine is pretty much the same as before, and the main difference now is the error subroutine. There is nothing in the program which prevents you from asking for an impossible record number. In the example in the manual, the record number is separately stored and read in, so that it can be compared to the number which you enter. I have chosen a different method. If the number that you pick for the record number is impossible, higher than the largest record number on the disk, then the error number 50 will be signalled, RECORD NOT PRESENT. In line 1020 this

```
200 OPEN15,8,15:OPEN6,8,6,"DATA"
220 INPUT "WHICH RECORD ";N:GOSUB1100:I
F N=0 THEN 310
240 PRINTCHR$(147):RESTORE:NT=1
250 FOR J=1TO5
260 READ TX$
270 PRINT#15,"P"CHR$(6)CHR$(L)CHR$(H)CH
R$(NT):GOSUB1000
280 INPUT#6,A$:GOSUB1000:PRINTTX$,A$
290 NT=NT+22:NEXT
300 GOTO220
310 CLOSE6:CLOSE15
320 PRINT"END":END
400 DATANAME,ADDRESS1,ADDRESS2,ADDRESS3
,ADDRESS4
500 PRINT"INSTRUCTIONS"
800 GETA$:IF A$=""THEN800
900 RETURN
1000 INPUT#15,A,B$,C,D:IF A<20THEN RETU
RN
1010 IF A<>50THENPRINTA,B$,C,D:STOP:RET
URN
1020 PRINT"INCORRECT RECORD NUMBER":RUN
1100 L=N:IF L>255THEN H=INT(L/256):L=L-
256*H
1110 RETURN
1500 NM$=LEFT$(NM$,20):RETURN
```

Fig. 5.6. Reading a relative file.

simply causes the program to print a message and then run again!
It's not an elegant solution, but it works. A better method will be
illustrated in Chapter 6.

More complications

These examples work nicely, but they are only illustrations for
learning purposes. For one thing, it's not very satisfactory that the
maximum record number is not placed on the disk file. For another
thing, you might not be able to remember record numbers. If you
want to find a name that starts with SIN, for example, this doesn't
help you to know which record number it is. It would be a lot more
useful if you could search the file for a given name rather than for a
given record number.

This is not something that you can do rapidly with relative files. You would have to load in each record, test it, and keep repeating this until you found the one that you wanted. The manual hints that this can be done by keeping a list of names and record numbers on another file. It suggests a serial file for the purpose. This is fine if the file has a fixed length, but if you want to extend the main file it's a bit of a pain trying to extend the serial file as well. We'll look at ways round these problems in the next chapter, which consists of a database program that uses relative and serial files.

Chapter Six
A Database Example - FILING CABINET

This chapter consists mainly of one long listing (Fig. 6.1) for a database type of program. The program is called FILING CABINET, and it allows you to specify five titles for the fields of your records. These field names are recorded on the disk, and will be used from then on. You can then enter information, add to information, read the data or select items as you please. These are the normal actions of a simple database. Looking at the length of the program, you might wonder how long a complicated program would be, but this *is* a simple version. There is no facility, for example, for changing a record. There is no facility for printing records in alphabetical order of any field. This is, you see, a skeleton database, which has been included to illustrate the use of the 1541 disk drive for this type of program. Once you have this program up and running, *and have completed reading this book*, you should be able to add whatever extra trimmings you need.

First principles

We shall start by looking at how the program works in outline. Three files are used, two relative files and one serial file. The serial file is used to keep a note of the names of the fields and the length of each field. When you first use the program for a new variety of file you will type these titles, and they stay with the file from then on unless you start another type of file on the same disk. If you want to use more than one FILING CABINET you must keep them on separate disks, with a copy of the program on each disk. One of the relative files is used to keep the records themselves, the other is used to keep a 'key'. The key file consists of the first three letters of the first field of each record. This allows you to pick a record by name, assuming that the names do not share the same first three letters.

```
10 PRINTCHR$(147)
20 F1=0
30 POKE53281,0:POKE53280,0
40 PRINTCHR$(5):REM WHITE
50 REM START KEY FILE
60 OPEN7,8,7,"KEY,L,"+CHR$(5)
70 CLOSE7
80 X$="NO SUCH FILENAME"
100 TT$="FILING CABINET":GOSUB1000
110 PRINT:PRINT"DO YOU NEED INSTRUCTIONS
 (Y/N)?":GOSUB1200
120 IF KY$="Y"THEN GOSUB 1400
130 GOSUB1600:TT$="MENU":GOSUB1000
140 PRINT:PRINT" 1. START NEW FILE."
150 PRINT:PRINT" 2. WRITE TO FILE."
160 PRINT:PRINT" 3. READ FILE."
170 PRINT:PRINT" 4. END PROGRAM."
180 PRINT:PRINT" PLEASE SELECT BY NUMBER
."
190 GOSUB1200:V%=VAL(KY$)
195 IF V%<1ORV%>4THENPRINT"1-4 ONLY, PLE
ASE TRY AGAIN":GOTO190
200 ON V%GOSUB2000,3000,4000,220
210 GOTO130
220 PRINT:PRINT"END OF PROGRAM":END
1000 D=INT((40-LEN(TT$))/2)
1010 PRINTTAB(D)CHR$(158);TT$
1020 RETURN
1200 GETKY$:IF KY$=""THEN 1200
1210 RETURN
1400 GOSUB1600:TT$="INSTRUCTIONS":GOSUB1
000:PRINT:PRINT
1410 PRINT"READ TEXT, THEN WRITE YOUR OW
N!"
1580 PRINT"PRESS SPACEBAR TO CONTINUE"
1590 GOSUB1200:RETURN
1600 PRINTCHR$(147):RETURN
1800 CLOSE5:CLOSE6
1810 CLOSE7:CLOSE15
1820 RETURN
1900 F1=1:PRINT:INPUT"FILE NAME, PLEASE
";FM$:GOSUB3500
1910 IF A=62 OR A=70THEN PRINTX$:FORZ=1T
O4000:NEXT:F1=0:RETURN
1920 RETURN
```

Fig. 6.1. The database program FILING CABINET.

```
2000 GOSUB1600:TT$="CREATE NEW FILE":GOS
UB1000
2010 PRINT:PRINT"PLEASE ENTER DATA AS RE
QUESTED "
2020 PRINT:PRINT" PRESS SPACEBAR TO STAR
T...":GOSUB1200:PRINT
2030 TL=2:FORJ=1TO5
2040 PRINT"TITLE ";J;" ":INPUT TL$(J):PR
INT"FIELD LENGTH- ";:INPUT LN(J)
2050 TL=TL+LN(J)+2:IF TL<255THEN NEXT:GO
TO2060
2055 PRINT"TOO LONG- PLEASE TRY SHORTER
FIELDS":GOTO2000
2060 PRINT:PRINT"WHAT FILENAME WOULD YOU
 LIKE":PRINT
2070 INPUT FM$:FM$=LEFT$(FM$,16)
2075 PRINT:PRINT"PLEASE WAIT FOR FILE PR
EPARATION"
2080 OPEN6,8,6,"@:TITLES,S,W"
2090 PRINT#6,TL:FORJ=1TO5
2100 PRINT#6,TL$(J):PRINT#6,LN(J):NEXT:C
LOSE6
2110 OPEN15,8,15:OPEN5,8,5,":"+FM$+",L,"
+CHR$(TL)
2120 PRINT#15,"P"CHR$(5)CHR$(0)CHR$(1)CH
R$(1)
2130 PRINT#5,"END":GOSUB10000:REM MAKE S
PACE FOR 256
2140 GOSUB1800
2150 V%=0:F1=1:RETURN
3000 GOSUB1600:TT$="WRITE TO FILE":GOSUB
1000:GOSUB1900:IF F1=0 THEN 3080
3010 PRINT:PRINT"DO YOU WANT TO-"
3020 PRINT:PRINTTAB(4)"1. START A FILE"
3030 PRINT:PRINTTAB(4)"2. CONTINUE A FIL
E"
3040 PRINT:PRINTTAB(4);"PLEASE SELECT BY
 NUMBER."
3050 GOSUB1200:V%=VAL(KY$)
3060 IF V%<1 OR V%>2 THEN PRINT"1 OR 2 O
NLY- PLEASE TRY AGAIN":GOTO3050
3070 ON V%GOSUB3100,3200
3080 GOSUB1800:V%=0:RETURN
3100 GOSUB1600:GOSUB7000:REM GET TITLES
3110 RN=1:GOSUB6000
```

Fig. 6.1. contd

```
3120 GOSUB5000:REM ENTRY
3130 V%=0:RETURN
3200 GOSUB1600:GOSUB7000:REM TITLES
3210 GOSUB3530:PRINT#15,"P"CHR$(7)CHR$(0
)CHR$(0)CHR$(1):GOSUB10000
3220 INPUT#7,N$:RN=1+VAL(N$):GOSUB6000
3230 GOSUB3550:GOSUB5000:REM ENTRY
3240 V%=0:RETURN
3500 OPEN15,8,15:OPEN6,8,6,":TITLES,S,R"
:GOSUB10000
3510 OPEN5,8,5,FM$:GOSUB10000
3520 RETURN
3530 CLOSE5:OPEN7,8,7,"KEY"
3540 RETURN
3550 CLOSE7:OPEN5,8,5,FM$
3560 RETURN
4000 GOSUB1600:TT$="READ FILE":GOSUB1900
:IF F1=0THEN 4320
4005 GOSUB7000:REM TITLES
4010 GOSUB1600:GOSUB1000:PRINT:PRINT "DO
YOU WANT TO-"
4020 PRINT:PRINTTAB(4)"1. READ ALL ITEMS
"
4030 PRINT:PRINTTAB(4)"2. READ SELECTED
ITEM":PRINT
4035 PRINTTAB(4)"3. RETURN TO MAIN MENU"
4040 PRINT:PRINTTAB(4)" PLEASE SELECT BY
NUMBER."
4050 GOSUB1200:V%=VAL(KY$)
4060 IF V%<1OR V%>3 THEN PRINT"1-3 ONLY,
PLEASE TRY AGAIN":GOTO4050
4070 ON V% GOSUB 4100,4200,4090
4080 IF V%<>0 THEN4000
4090 GOSUB1800:V%=0:RETURN
4100 GOSUB1600:GOSUB3530:PRINT#15,"P"CHR
$(7)CHR$(1)CHR$(0)CHR$(1)
4110 INPUT#7,A$
4120 RX=VAL(A$):GOSUB3550
4130 FOR RN=1TORX:GOSUB6000
4140 PRINT#15,"P"CHR$(5)CHR$(L)CHR$(H)CH
R$(1)
4150 GOSUB6100:REM READ FILE#5 AND PRINT
4160 PRINT:PRINT"PRESS SPACEBAR FOR NEXT
, Q TO QUIT."
4170 GOSUB1200:IF KY$<>"Q"THEN NEXT
```

Fig. 6.1. contd

```
4180 GOTO4320:REM CLOSE AND RETURN
4200 GOSUB1600:PRINT"TYPE NAME PLEASE...
"
4210 INPUT NM$:ID$=LEFT$(NM$,3):GOSUB353
0
4220 PRINT#15,"P"CHR$(7)CHR$(1)CHR$(0)CH
R$(1)
4230 INPUT#7,A$:RX=VAL(A$):FORRN=2TORX+1
4240 GOSUB6000:PRINT#15,"P"CHR$(7)CHR$(L
)CHR$(H)CHR$(1)
4250 INPUT#7,A$:IF ID$=LEFT$(A$,3)THEN42
70
4260 NEXT:GOSUB3550:GOTO4350
4270 RN=RN-1:GOSUB6000:GOSUB3550:GOSUB61
00
4290 PRINT:PRINT"PRESS SPACEBAR FOR NEXT
, Q TO QUIT"
4300 GOSUB1200:IF KY$<>"Q"THEN4200
4320 GOSUB1800:J%=0:RETURN
4350 PRINT"NO SUCH FILE-PLEASE TRY AGAIN
":FORZ=1TO4000:NEXT
4360 GOTO4200:REM TRY AGAIN
5000 GOSUB1600:PRINT:PRINT:N1=1
5010 PRINT"ITEM ";RN:FORJ=1TO5
5020 PRINTTL$(J),:INPUT NM$:GOSUB5080:IF
 LEFT$(NM$,1)="X"THEN 5070
5025 CLOSE7
5030 GOSUB6000:PRINT#15,"P"CHR$(5)CHR$(L
)CHR$(H)CHR$(N1)
5040 PRINT#5,NM$:N1=N1+2+LN(J):GOSUB1000
0
5050 IF J=1THEN GOSUB 5200:REM UPDATE KE
Y
5060 NEXT:RN=RN+1:GOTO5000
5070 RETURN
5080 NM$=LEFT$(NM$,LN(J)):RETURN
5200 GOSUB3530:PRINT#15,"P"CHR$(7)CHR$(1
)CHR$(0)CHR$(1)
5205 PRINT#7,RN:RN=RN+1:GOSUB6000
5207 PRINT#15,"P"CHR$(7)CHR$(L)CHR$(H)CH
R$(1)
5210 PRINT#7,LEFT$(NM$,3):RN=RN-1:GOSUB1
0000
5220 GOSUB3550:RETURN
```

Fig. 6.1. contd

```
6000 L=RN: IF L>255THEN H=INT(L/256):L=L-
256*H
6010 RETURN
6100 N1=1:FORJ=1TO5
6110 PRINT#15,"P"CHR$(5)CHR$(L)CHR$(H)CH
R$(N1)
6120 INPUT#5,NM$:PRINTNM$
6130 N1=N1+2+LN(J)
6140 NEXT
6150 RETURN
7000 INPUT#6,TL:FOR J=1TO5
7010 INPUT#6,TL$(J)
7020 INPUT#6,LN(J):NEXT
7030 CLOSE6:RETURN
10000 INPUT#15,A,B$,C,D
10010 IF A<20THEN 10050
10020 IF A=50THEN 10050
10030 IF A=62THEN10050
10035 IF A=70 THEN 10050
10040 PRINTB$:STOP:RETURN
10050 RETURN
```

Fig. 6.1. contd

You could use the first two and the last letter as another way of identification, or devise other combinations to suit yourself. As I said, this is a skeleton program, and it's yours to trim to shape and pad out as you please. One thing that we have to be *very* careful about is that the 1541 does not like having two relative files open at the same time. This causes NO CHANNEL error reports, and other complications.

When the program runs a KEY file is opened, and you are presented with the main menu. The first time that you use the program on a disk you should go for the START NEW FILE option. This allows you to choose five titles for the fields of your record, and asks you for the length of each field. These names and figures will be recorded and used forever after, so you should plan them carefully. Figure 6.2 shows a typical display. After entering the fields and lengths, you are prompted for a filename. You can choose anything you like, as long as it has 16 characters or less and is not KEY or TITLES. The reason, of course, is that these filenames are used for other files. Perhaps you might like to add a line 2072, which rejected these names as filenames and asked again.

TITLE 1 SURNAME
FIELD LNGTH— 20

TITLE 2 FORENAME
FIELD LNGTH— 15

TITLE 3 DATE OF BIRTH (DDMMYY)
FIELD LNGTH— 6

TITLE 4 OCCUPATION
FIELD LNGTH— 30

TITLE 5 PHONE NUMBER
FIELD LENGTH— 12

WHAT FILENAME WOULD YOU LIKE
?WORKFORCE

Fig. 6.2. A typical screen display after the entry of titles and field lengths.

Once the filename has been typed and RETURN pressed, the main file is opened with the name you have selected. The pointer is then moved to record number 256 and the word END placed there. This takes time, and a 'Please wait' message is printed to remind you. At several places in the program the disk will be busy and you may have to wait for it. When the file has been created, the program returns to the menu.

You can now type into your file by choosing the WRITE TO FILE option. You will then be asked for the filename. This is to ensure that the correct file is identified. If you choose the wrong name, you will be informed and the menu will reappear. When you use the correct filename, this brings up a new menu in which your choice is either to START A FILE or to CONTINUE A FILE. If you have just entered the field names you will be starting a file, and you would also pick this option if you wanted to wipe out and replace a file of the same name. In this option, you will be prompted by the field names (such as ADDRESS, NAME, etc.) to type data. The data will be chopped to the field size that you have specified, and recorded. There is a noticeable pause following the first name in each field. This is because the first three letters of this field are also recorded on the KEY file. Don't rush your typing after you press RETURN on this first field. You will also find that the disk spins at other places while you enter data, and you have to wait until the screen cursor is visible again before you can continue typing. To end the entry, you type X, or a name that starts with X. If this is inconvenient, change it (line 5020)! If you have a file already created, you can use the other write option to extend the file. You don't have to input the record number, because this is recorded with the KEY file and the file will be extended with no gaps.

If you select the READ option from the main menu you will once again be presented with another menu, after checking for the filename. This time the choice is to list all of the names or pick a name. If you choose to list all names, the disk starts to work hard and a complete record is printed on the screen. You can press the spacebar to get the next record until the end of the file, or you can press Q to return to the start of this menu with the FILENAME prompt. If you choose to select a name, you are asked to type the name. This will be the name of the first field item. Only the first three letters are important in the program as it is organised at present. The program then opens the KEY file, and looks for these letters. Since this is a much shorter file than the main file, the search is quick. When the letters are found, the record number is calculated and the main file is read to produce the record that you want. At present there is no facility to produce more than one record with the same identifying letters, and the program will always pick the first record that answers the description. Once again, it's your program – change it as you want. If you ask for a name that does not appear in the file, then you will be advised and asked to try again. That's it!

The program in detail

Now for the hard work. There are a lot of points in this program which are important. If you try to design your own database programs you will need to know what the 1541 disk drive does, and this listing reveals a lot that isn't exactly made clear by the manual, and which is not so easy to illustrate by short examples. No matter how much you may hate looking at other people's programs, then, it will be useful to study this one so that you can appreciate reasons. Unless you do so, you can waste a lot of time looking at the 1541's inscrutable error messages and wondering why they arise.

The program is built round a core and a set of subroutines. A lot of the programming is straightforward BASIC, and I have made no use of fancy colour or screen presentation effects – there's quite enough to type as it is. I'll concentrate on the explanations that relate to the use of the disk drive, rather than explain everything in detail. In other words, I'm assuming that you knew a reasonable amount of BASIC before you bought a disk drive.

Lines 10–80 are concerned with initial values of constants and setting screen display. The relative file KEY is also opened. By using this opening statement at this point, we can then use OPEN7,8,7, "KEY" in future commands. The variable X$ is used to deliver an error message at a place in one of the subroutines, and the program starts in earnest in line 100. This prints a title, centred by the GOSUB1000, and asks if you need instructions. The GOSUB1200 is a GET KY$ routine which will wait for a key to be pressed. Any key apart from Y will cause the instructions to be skipped. I have not written detailed instructions, because these are just another load of typing. You can type your own instructions when you have modified the program for your own use.

Line 130 clears the screen (GOSUB1600) and then prints the menu. You are asked to select by number, using the GET KY$ subroutine and converting to number form with VAL. This number is assigned to V% (an integer) and tested. If the range is acceptable, then line 200 carries out the choice. In the course of this choice, the value of V% can be changed. This can cause another subroutine to run when the RETURN is used, so each subroutine ends with V%=0 to prevent this. Line 210 ensures that the menu is repeated unless you have picked the END PROGRAM option. The subroutines then carry out the main actions. This is important, because it makes the program very easy to change. Practically all the subroutines that you might need for your own 'custom' version are listed, so if you know in detail what each subroutine does, making your own version is relatively easy.

The creation subroutine

The subroutine that starts in line 2000 creates a new file. This will wipe out any other file that has been created with this program on the same disk, which is why it's useful to have several copies of the program on different disks. The loop that starts in line 2030 gets title names for each field, and also a length number. The length number is not tested, and it might be useful to reject lengths of less than 1 or more than, say, 50. Each title and length is assigned to an array, using TL$ for the title and LN for the length of field. If the total field length, allowing for spaces and carriage returns, is too long, then you will have to start again. This test is made in line 2050. If all is well, then you are asked for a filename in line 2060. Once again, it might be useful to test this to make sure that the names KEY and

TITLES were not used. Line 2080 then opens a serial file for writing. By using @ in the filename of TITLES, any previous file of this name is deleted. The total length of record, each title name and each field length figure are then recorded in this serial file, and the file is closed. Line 2110 then opens the command channel, and channel 5 is opened for a relative file whose name is the one that you have selected, FM$. The record length has already been calculated as TL, and this can be included in the OPEN statement. In line 2120, the pointer is placed at a position for the 256th record, and END is printed to make room. This causes filing to operate faster in future, and it would have been an advantage to do the same with the KEY file early in the program. Try it!

It takes time to allocate space for 256 records, so a message to this effect is printed in line 2075. Line 2949 calls a subroutine that closes all files, and line 2150 sets 'flag' variables and returns. Your titles and field lengths are now recorded, and the files are set up and ready to use.

Writing to the file

Selecting the WRITE option in the main menu leads to line 3000. The filename for the data file is checked, and if all is well another menu is presented. This gives the options of starting a file of data or continuing a file. If the START FILE option is selected, this will replace any existing file. The START option then leads to line 3100. This uses GOSUB7000 to read the serial file, TITLES, so that the titles of each field are read into the array TL$ and the lengths into LN. This is important because whatever you enter will have to be cut to the correct size if it exceeds the allocated field length. For a new file, the record number RN will start with a value of 1, and the subroutine at 6000 converts this number into H,L form. The main entry is then carried out (line 3120) by calling the entry subroutine at line 5000. When entry is complete (X is typed), line 3130 sets V% to 0, and returns.

When the CONTINUE A FILE option is selected, the subroutine starts at 3200. This reads the titles once again, but then has to find the correct value of record number RN to extend the file. This process starts in line 3210. The GOSUB3530 closes the main file channel (#5) and opens the KEY file channel, #7. This has to be done, because you can't PRINT# or INPUT# with both relative files open. The pointer is then put to the first record of the KEY file. This is used, as we'll see later, to hold the maximum record number so that this quantity can be read in line 3220 and converted back to number form. We then add 1 to prepare for the next record, and use GOSUB600 to convert into H,L form. In line 3230, the GOSUB3550 closes channel 7 and reopens channel 5, the main data channel. The program then makes use of the entry subroutine at line 500 again to get another set of data. When this is complete, line 3240 sets V% to zero, and returns.

Reading the file

The file reading option in the main menu once again causes a prompt for a filename, and the file is checked by the subroutine in line 1900. The new menu that is then presented gives the options of reading all files or a selected file. If the ALL FILES option is picked, the subroutine which starts at line 4100 is run. The first three lines of this subroutine are used to read the maximum record number from the KEY file. As before, this involves closing #5, opening #7, reading the value, and then closing #7 and opening #5 again. The value of maximum record number is assigned to RX, and this is used as the terminating value in a loop which starts in line 4130. In each pass of the loop, RN is assigned to a number, the H,L values are found, and these are used to position the pointer in the main file. Line 4150 then calls the subroutine that reads the file and prints the data. After each read, a PRESS SPACEBAR TO CONTINUE step is used to prevent the data scrolling out of sight before you have had time to read it. A 'quit' option is also included so that you can stop when you have had enough.

Using the SELECTED ITEM option leads to line 4200. You are asked to type the name that you want, meaning the name of the first field of the record. The variable ID$ is then used to hold the first three letters of this name. Channel 7 is then selected by the subroutine at 3530, and the pointer is placed at the start of the KEY file. Line 4230 gets the first item in this file, which is the maximum number of records. The rest of the file, starting at record number 2, consists of the first three letters of names, and so this file can now be searched. The loop starts at the end of line 4230, and uses the maximum record number RX+1 as its terminator. The '+1' is needed because the KEY file always contains one more item than the main file. This is the maximum record number which is stored at the start of the file. The file then goes from record number 2 to one more than the value of record number that is recorded. Lines 4240 and 4250 set the pointer for each value of RN, read the KEY file and compare the letters. If a match is found, the loop drops out to line 4270 (*not* good practice!) and RN=RN−1 restores the correct value of RN for the main file. If no match is found at the end of the loop, the files are swopped over (#7 closed, #5 opened), a message is printed, and the subroutine starts again. If the name is found the files also have to be swopped, and the reading subroutine at 6100 is used to read the full file entry. Lines 4290, 4300 then give you a chance to get another entry or to quit. The subroutine ends in 4320 by closing files, setting V% to zero, and returning to the menu.

The entry subroutine

The entry subroutine starts at line 5000. The correct channels must have been opened by the time this is called, and this is something you must ensure if you extend the program. In addition, the subroutine will use whatever value of RN is passed to it by the main program. This value is printed as an item number in line 5010, and a loop starts to read in field values. In each pass of the loop the title for the file is printed, and then you must input a value (name or number). The entry is chopped to size by the GOSUB5080, and the program checks for the entry of X, which terminates the procedure. Line 5025 ensures that channel#7 is closed, because you can't use two open relative files. Lines 5030 and 5040 then place the entry on disk (or, more correctly, in a buffer). The pointer is set, using H and L values, and with N1 as the position in the record. The number N1 is calculated from the field lengths, allowing for the added carriage return and a space. Line 5050 detects if this is the first field, because this is the key field. If so, the subroutine at 5200 is called to print the record number and the first three letters of the first field into the KEY file. We'll look at that later. The loop ends in line 5060, and the record number is incremented. The GOTO5000 then makes this action repeat until an X is entered. The entry of X causes line 5070 to return to the calling point.

The subroutine at 5200 is closely related to the writing routine, because it writes on the KEY file for each first field in the main file. Line 5200 selects the correct file (close #5, open #7), and places the pointer at record number 1. Line 5205 then prints RN in this position, and the number RN has to be incremented. The incremented value is then used to place the pointer in the KEY file and print the first three letters of the key field (line 5210). The RN value is then restored, the files are also restored (#7 closed, #5 opened), and the routine returns.

Reading, and some loose ends

The general reading routine starts in line 6100. Once again, N1 is used for position in the record and the loop is used to read each field. Line 6110 sets the pointer, and line 6120 reads in the data and prints it. Line 6130 updates the value of N12, using the same formula as was used when files were written. At the end of the loop the routine returns. This is one of the most straightforward of the file-using routines.

The routine at line 7000 reads the serial file so as to obtain the names of the fields. In the program, this subroutine has been used rather too much. I have assumed that the program is used once and then switched off, so that the titles have to be read for each use. In fact, once you have read the titles they stay until you run the program again. You might want to put a test at every point where GOSUB7000 is used. A suitable test would be:

IF NM$(1)="" THEN GOSUB7000

which would call the subroutine only if it were needed. This will save a lot of time and disk use.

The error routines are located at 10000. These follow the lines that we discussed in Chapter 5, but error 70 is also tested. This is the NO CHANNEL error, and it seems to occur if there is no file or if the file is of the wrong name. The main use for this is in the subroutine at line 1900. This uses a 'flag' variable F1 which is initially set at a value of 1. When you type the file name, FM$, the subroutine at 3500 is called. This opens files, but the order of opening is *very* important. The command channel #15 must be opened before #5 can be opened, and the OPEN5,8,5,"FM$" *must* be the last opened. The reason is that we are going to use the error message from this step to set the flag F1. If you put this command in the first of the lines, 3500, then its error message will have disappeared when the serial file is opened. If the filename is wrong, there will be an error which will be number 62 or 70 (I always found 70). This causes the program to print the string X$, and wait. The flag is set to zero, and the subroutine returns. This value of F1 is then used to prevent any file action in the subroutines, either for writing or for reading.

That's all there is to it. Taken as a whole it looks rather intimidating, but when you split it into core and subroutines, as it was when it was written, it looks a lot simpler. It's yours now. Modify it as you wish, but please don't sell it or publish it as your own work!

Chapter Seven
Printers

Whenever your use of a computer extends beyond playing games that other people have written, there are two additions to your computer equipment that you will urgently want. One of these is a disk system, and that's a topic that has filled the first six chapters of this book. The next must be a printer. In many cases, the printer has an even higher priority than the disk system.

The reasons for using a printer are obvious if you use the machine for business purposes. You can hardly expect your accountant or your income-tax inspector to look at accounts that can be shown only on the screen. It would be a total waste of time if you kept your stock records with a computer and then had to write down each change on a piece of paper, copying from the display on the screen. For all of these purposes, and particularly for word processing, the printer is an essential part of the computer system. Output on paper is referred to as 'hard copy', and this hard copy is essential if the computer is to be of any use in business applications. For word processing uses, it's not enough just to have a printer – you need a printer with a high-quality output, with characters as clear as those of a first-class electric typewriter.

Even if your computer is never used for any kind of business purpose you can run up against the need for a printer. If you use, modify or write programs, the printer can pay for itself in terms of your time. Trying to trace what a program does from a listing that you can see only a few lines at a time on the screen is totally frustrating. Quite apart from anything else, the BASIC of the C'64 relies a lot on the use of GOTO for loops, and you might have to list a dozen different pieces of a program just to find where one GOTO could lead you to. The problem is even worse if you write your own programs. Even a very modest program may need a hundred lines of BASIC, especially when the C'64 permits only such short lines. Trying to check a program of a hundred lines when you may be able to see only a dozen or so at a time is like bailing out a leaky boat with a teaspoon. With a printer attached to your C'64, however, you can print out the whole listing and then examine it at your leisure. If you design your programs the way you ought to, using a 'core' and subroutines, then you can print each subroutine on a separate piece of paper. In this way you can keep a note of each different subroutine, with variable names noted. On each sheet you can write what the subroutine does, what quantities are represented by the variable names, and how it is used. If you have a utility program that allows you to merge subroutines, you can then construct programs painlessly using your library of tested subroutines.

Printer types

Granted, then, that the use of a printer is a high priority for the really serious computer user, what sort of printers are available? The C'64 in its natural state allows only Commodore printers to be attached, but thanks to the ingenuity of a great number of independent suppliers you can, for a small sum, now attach almost any printer you like to the C'64. This opens up the way for the use of any of the printers which are offered at such attractive prices in the magazines.

Printers that are used with small computers will use one of the mechanisms that are listed in Fig. 7.1. Of these, the impact *dot-*

Dot matrix
impact
thermal
electrostatic

Type impact
type stalk
daisywheel

Plotters
graphics printers
X-Y plotters

Ink-jet
single colour
multicolour

Fig. 7.1. A list of printer mechanism types.

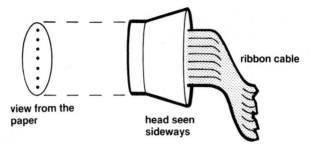

Fig. 7.2. Illustrating a dot-matrix printhead.

matrix type is the most common. A dot matrix printer creates each character out of a set of dots, and when you look at the print closely you can see the dot structure. The printhead of the dot-matrix printer consists of a set of tiny electromagnets, each of which acts on a set of needles that are arranged in a vertical line (Fig. 7.2). By firing these needles at an inked ribbon which is placed between the head and the paper, dots can be marked on the paper. Each character is printed by firing some needles, moving the head slightly, then firing another set of needles, and so on until the character shape is completely drawn (Fig. 7.3). The most common pattern of dots for low-cost printers is the 7×5, meaning that the characters can be

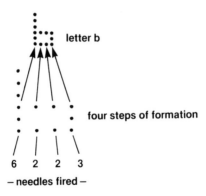

Fig. 7.3. How a 7×5 dot matrix head creates a character.

made out of up to seven dots in height and up to five in width. This implies that the head moves across the paper in five steps to print each character, and that up to seven needles can be fired. Using a 7×5 structure gives characters which are readable, but not good-looking. The dots are very evident, and some of the letters are misshapen. You will find, for example, that lower case letters lack 'descenders'. This means the tails on letters y,g,p,q will either be missing or will be on the same level as the foot of other letters. When this print is used for listings which are in upper-case only, there is no problem. You would not, however, use a printer of this class to print letters or other documents that anyone else would have to read.

Rather better results can be obtained if the number of needles in the printhead is increased. Using 9×9 (nine needles, nine steps across) or 15×9 heads can create much better-looking characters, lower-case or upper-case. Another advantage of these printheads is that the characters are not limited to the ordinary letters of the alphabet and the numbers. Foreign characters can usually be printed, and it is possible to print Arabic script or to make up your own character set, for example.

Most of the dot-matrix printers are *impact* types. This means what it says, that the paper is marked by the impact of a needle on an inked ribbon which hits the paper. There are also *thermal* and *electrostatic* dot-matrix printers. These use needles, but the needles do not move. Instead, the needles are used to affect a special type of paper. In the electrostatic printer (such as the ZX printer) the needles are used to pass sparks to the paper, removing a thin coating of metal from the black backing paper. The thermal type of printer uses hot needles to make marks on heat-sensitive paper. Both of these printers require expensive special paper and are unsuitable for serious business purposes, so we won't spend any time on them here. If you want a cheap printer for listings, there are better methods.

The ultimate in print-quality at the moment is provided by the *daisywheel printer*. This uses a typewriter approach, with the letters and other characters placed on stalks round a wheel. The principle is that the wheel spins to get the letter that you want at the top, and then a small hammer hits the back of the letter, pressing it against the ribbon and on to the paper. Because this is exactly the same way as a typewriter produces text, the quality of print is very high. It's also possible now to buy a combination of typewriter and daisywheel printer. This looks like a typewriter, with a normal typewriter keyboard, but has an interface connection for a computer. You can use it as a typewriter, and then connect it to the computer and use it as a printer. Machines of this sort are made by leading typewriter manufacturers such as Silver Reed, Brother, Triumph-Adler, Smith-Corona, and others. If you need a typewriter as well as a printer, then this type of machine is an obvious choice.

The third kind of mechanism that we shall look at here is the *graphics printer*. This is a remarkable mechanism which uses four miniature ball pens to mark the paper direct, with no ribbon. It can be used for graphics work, and when it is used as a printer the letters are drawn rather than printed. Because four pens are used, the markings can be in four different colours. Printers of this type are not expensive (as printers go) and can be very useful, particularly if you want graphics output in colour.

Another type of printer that is now becoming available is the *ink-jet printer*, which operates by shooting fine jets of ink at the paper. This one shares the disadvantage of the thermal and the electrostatic types in that you get only one copy. Impact printers all have the great advantage that you can get an extra copy by using a sheet of carbon paper and another sheet of plain paper. You can also buy listing paper which has a built-in carbon, or which uses the NCR (No Carbon Required) principle to produce two copies.

Interfaces

The printer has to be connected by a cable to the computer so that signals can be passed in each direction. The computer will pass to the printer the signals that make the printer produce characters on the paper, but the printer must also be able to pass signals to the computer. This is because the printer operates much more slowly than the computer. Unless the printer contains a large memory buffer, so that it can store all the signals from the computer and then get to work on them at its own pace, some sort of 'handshaking' is needed. This means that the printer will accept as many signals as its memory will take, and then send out a signal to the computer which makes the computer hang up. When the printer has completed a number of characters (one line, one thousand, or possibly just one character) it changes the 'handshake' signal and the computer sends another batch. This continues until all of the text has been printed. This can mean that you don't have the use of the computer until the printer has finished. Printers can be very slow, particularly daisywheel and plotter types. Even the fastest dot-matrix printers can make you wait for a minute or more for a listing.

Two types of interface are used by practically all printers. These are classed as serial or parallel. A *parallel* printer is connected to the computer by a cable which uses a large number of separate strands. Since each character in ASCII code uses seven signals, the parallel printer sends these along seven separate strands – many printers can use an eighth signal and this is usually sent as well. In addition, there are cable strands for the 'handshake' signals. The best-known, and most-used variety of parallel connection is called Centronics, after the printer manufacturer which first used it. Practically all of the popular printers use this type of parallel interface.

The *serial* interface sends the signals out one at a time. This means that at least seven signals have to be sent for each character, and in practice this must be ten or eleven, to allow for 'start and stop' signals which are used to mark where the signals for each character start and stop. This system uses less cabling because only two strands need to be used for signals, and the cables can be longer because there's no risk of one signal interfacing with another. The standard system is called RS-232. Printers can be obtained with RS-232, but seldom as standard, and often only as an extra costing up to £50. The Commodore 64 uses a serial system, but it is not one of the standard forms, so only Commodore printers can be connected unless you attach an interface. We'll deal later with this point. For now, we'll look at just one of the range of Commodore printers that can be attached to your C'64.

The VIC 1515 printer

Of all the printers that can attach directly to the C'64, the VIC 1515 is the lowest priced, and this is the printer that was supplied with my C'64. It is no longer listed, and the current equivalent is the 1525. Nevertheless, there are still lots of 1515s being sold, and the details of operation should apply to the 1525 also. The advantage of the later type of printer is that paper is much easier to obtain. Though the 1515 uses 'ordinary' listing paper, this is of an odd size and must be perforated. Like many small printers, the 1515 uses 'pin feed', meaning that the paper is pulled and located by a set of pins that engage in holes at the side of the paper. The VIC 1515 requires paper of no more than eight inches wide. If, however, you remove the paper stops which are screwed in place where the paper is loaded into the printer, you can use standard eight and a half inch width paper. This makes the printer a better buy if you are short of money! The main cost after that is ribbons. These use twin spools, and the length of ribbon is very short so they have a comparatively short life. It's better to buy them in bulk, at least a dozen at a time.

The VIC 1515 is connected to the C'64 or to the disk drive by a cable which uses the same sort of six-pin DIN plug as the C'64 disk drive. If you have no disk drive on your C'64, this cable plugs into the DIN socket that lies next to the cassette socket. If you have a disk drive connected, you will find that there is a spare socket of this type on the disk drive. The other end of the cable plugs into a similar socket at the back of the printer. Just next to this socket is a small switch which is labelled '4 5 T'. This allows you to select auto-test (T) so that the printer will run over its set of characters when you switch it on. The numbers allow you to select a 'filenumber' of 4 or 5. This must be opened in the usual way, and you can use the number in PRINT# commands. The usual number to select is 4.

Having connected your printer, then, feed some paper into it. This can be a bit of a struggle, and it needs a lot of shuffling to make sure that the paper engages correctly with the pins. Once this has been done and the paper clamped in place, select T with the switch and switch on the printer. You should see the printer characters appearing until the printer is switched off. Try to use the cover on the printer at all times, because the VIC 1515 is unbelievably noisy if this cover is removed.

Listings are the main reason for using this printer, so we'll look at how it's done. You must have the program that you want to list in the memory of the computer. You then type:

OPEN3,4 (press RETURN)
CMD3 (press RETURN)

and then LIST (press RETURN). The program will then list on the printer instead of on the screen (which is the effect of the CMD3). At the end of the listing you have to type PRINT#3 to cancel the CMD3, and if you are not using the printer again you add CLOSE3. If you want to start the listing with a comment, you can do this *before* you use CMD3. Suppose, for example, you want to print the words VERSION 2.1, then you will need to type PRINT#3,"VERSION 2.1" and press RETURN. You can then use CMD3, and then LIST. The effect of CMD3 is to send everything that would normally go to the screen to the printer instead.

Very often, you may want a program to produce printed output with the screen being used only for messages to the operator. This is the most common way of using the printer and the screen in business programs, for example, and it can also be of advantage for a lot of other types of program that deal with data. You will need to have opened the printer channel early in the program by using OPEN3,4 (assuming that you have set the switch on the printer to 4). Wherever you want printed material, you will need to use a PRINT#3," in place of the PRINT" that you would use for the screen. There are utility programs for the C'64 that allow you to program the keys at the right-hand side of the keyboard (yes, they *can* be used!) so that one press of a key can enter a complete phrase like PRINT#3,", and this can save a lot of time when you are programming.

```
10 REM THIS IS THE NORMAL UPPER CASE
20 REM PRINT OF THE VIC 1515
```

Fig. 7.4. The normal upper-case text of the VIC 1515 printer.

Figure 7.4 shows the normal text of the VIC 1515. This is acceptable for a listing, and all of the characters will appear in upper-case when the printer is used in this way. To obtain a printout of anything that is typed in lower-case, you have to send an appropriate command to the printer. For listings that were made in lower-case, this consists of OPEN3,4,7. The 7 is the 'cursor down' command code, and it will cause the printer to operate in lower-case. The REMs that were in upper-case in this example have not been printed. This demonstrates that lower-case can be printed, but the appearance is not pleasing (Fig. 7.5). Lower-case print commands

```
10   this is in lower case
20   to demonstrate how this looks on the 1515.
     g y d p q letters
```

Fig. 7.5. The lower-case of the VIC 1515.

have to include CHR$(17) before the text to place the printer into 'cursor down' mode.

The graphics characters of the C'64 can also be printed, and this is the main advantage of using the 1515 or any of its later counterparts. If you use the CLR key, for example, placed between quotes, then the symbol that appears on the screen is the heart shape. This will be produced by the 1515 printer, but not by any non-Commodore printer. A further bonus of the 1515 is that it can print in larger-than-normal letters. If you OPEN3,4, and then use PRINT#3,CHR$(14), you can then list in double-width characters, as Fig. 7.6 illustrates.

```
10  REM DOUBLE WIDTH CHARACTERS
20  REM OF THE VIC 1515
```

Fig. 7.6. Double-width characters on the VIC 1515, using CHRS(14).

The double-width characters can be cancelled by using PRINT#3,CHR$(15). Reverse field (white on black) and graphics printing is also possible. The graphics printing allows you to print patterns by directly controlling which of the printhead needles are fired at the paper.

The range of Commodore printers is fairly large, and you may very well feel that there is no need for you to look at any other printer types. The non-standard interface is a disadvantage, however. Most computers can make use of printers which have the Centronics parallel interface, and it is a great advantage to have this. For one thing, it allows you to use the most popular printers that are the best value for money. For another thing, if you ever change machines you will not have to part with a printer which uses a Centronics interface because it will work with practically all other computers. The Commodore printers are modified versions of the popular printers designed to work with Commodore machines only. Fortunately, it is comparatively easy to convert your C'64 so that it can be connected to a Centronics style of interface.

The Centronics interface

Several suppliers advertise Centronics interfaces for the C'64. These consist of a cable which plugs into the socket at the back left-hand side of the C'64 and which has a Centronics printer socket at the other end. This is not enough for printing, however, and you need a program in machine code to send the correct signals to the printer. This can be supplied on cassette or on disk. At the time of writing, the 'best buy' in such interfaces was from Microport, 7 Clydesdale Close, Borehamwood, Herts. WD6 2SD, at a price of around £26 for the cassette version. If you want the disk version, or you think the price may have changed since this was written, you should contact Mick Bignell at the above address.

When the program runs, machine code is placed into high memory, and the C'64 will drive a printer with a Centronics interface. This does not mean that the graphics can be reproduced, so if you insist on using graphics in your programs you should make them of the CHR$(nn) variety rather than by using the graphics keys. In this book, for example, the listings have been reproduced on an Epson RX80 printer. This uses a 9×9 matrix for characters, so that the appearance of the characters is better. In addition, the Epson can operate in 'emphasised' mode. In this printing mode each dot is struck twice, but the head is shifted slightly between dots. This causes the dots to look almost joined up, and makes the appearance of the print much more acceptable.

A problem that you are bound to run up against when you use any non-Commodore printer is that of line feed and carriage return. A lot of computers send out only one code number, the carriage return code (13), at the end of a line. Other machines send both the line feed (code 10) and carriage return codes. Printers are arranged, therefore, so that either possibility can be catered for by a switch. If you connect your printer and find that everything is printed on one line (as may happen when the C'64 is driving the printer), then don't return the printer. Just look in the manual and find the switch that alters the line feed setting. If, on the other hand you are using another computer with your printer and you find that each line is double-spaced, then this switch will have to be set to the opposite position.

The Epson RX80

The Epson range of printers has for a long time been the most popular range of moderately-priced printers, offering good print quality at reasonable prices. The RX80 is the latest in this line, but if you are offered a second-hand MX80, then this also is a good buy. A particular feature of the Epson range is that the print heads can easily be replaced when they wear out. My old Epson MX80 is just beginning to show signs of head-wear after printing half a million words, so it might not be a problem for you!

The standard version of the RX80 uses pin-feed, but the RX80F/T can take any form of paper, including rolls. You have to pay extra for a paper roll holder, but if you are handy with wood this is something that you could easily make for yourself. The advantage of using the F/T version is that plain, unperforated paper rolls are very much cheaper to buy, and it also means that you can use plain paper sheets if you want to. When you use a lot of paper for listings this can be a great saving. Paper width of four to ten inches in pin-feed can be used, so you can buy whatever paper size is on offer. If you use the F/T option, you can then buy the teletype rolls which are eight and a half inches wide.

The RX80 offers a full set of upper- or lower-case letters, and you don't have to go through any elaborate antics to select which one

```
10 REM USING RX80 IN NORMAL MODE
20 REM WHICH PRINTS AT MAXIMUM SPEED
```

Fig. 7.7. The normal upper-case characters of the Epson RX80.

you want. Figure 7.7 shows the normal upper-case letters of the RX80, as you would use them for a listing. The print speed is very fast, and most listings will be completed in under a minute. Figure 7.8 shows the lower-case letters, which were produced by selecting

```
10 rem lower case on the screen
20 rem can also be produced on the printer.
```

Fig. 7.8. The lower-case characters of the Epson RX80.

```
10 REM THIS SHOWS THE EMPHASISED
20 REM STYLE OF PRINT OF THE RX80
```

Fig. 7.9. The emphasised print of the RX80.

lower-case before typing the program. This is made possible by the machine code which is part of the interface. Figure 7.9 shows the 'emphasised' type of the MX80. This is achieved by typing PRINT#3,CHR$(27)CHR$(69) (press RETURN) before listing. The emphasised print can be cancelled by using PRINT#3, CHR$(27)CHR$(70). These commands can be used in programs, so that you can print normal, condensed, emphasised, double-width, and all of the other varieties, under program control. This makes it very easy to produce good headings, produce words in bold type or italics, and to underline. For a lot of word processing actions, the RX80 can be a very satisfactory low-cost alternative to a daisywheel.

Switch 1		
Position	ON	OFF
1	Condensed	Pica (print size)
2	Graphics	Control code
3	No buzzer	Buzzer on (end of paper)
4	12 inch	11 inch (form length)
5	Not detected	Detected (paper end)
6	Selects from international	
7	character set of	
8	eight languages	
Switch 2		
Position	ON	OFF
1	Slashed	Non-slashed (zero)
2	Control pin	Not fixed
3	Line feed	No line feed (with C/R)
4	Skip	Don't skip (perforation)

Fig. 7.10. List of RX80 switch settings.

Each of the letter codes will be preceded by CHR$(27), the ESC code. Some of the CHR$(number) codes can be used alone – consult the manual for details.

Code	Effect
J	Adjust line spacing in 1/216 inch units.
M	Elite size characters.
P	Pica size characters.
CHR$(14)	Enlarged print.
CHR$(20)	Cancel enlarged print.
W	Second enlarged print mode.
CHR$(15)	Condensed print.
CHR$(18)	Cancel condensed print.
_	Underline on/off switch.
E	Set emphasised mode.
F	Cancel emphasised mode.
G	Double strike mode.
H	Cancel double strike mode.
S	Superscript/subscript switch.
T	Cancel superscript/subscript.
CHR$(8)	Backspace.
CHR$(4)	Alternate character set.
CHR$(5)	Cancel alternate character set.
m	Choose graphics or control characters.
0	1/8 inch line spacing.
1	7/72 inch line spacing.
2	1/6 inch line spacing.
3	Set spacing in 1/216 inch units.
A	Set line spacing in 1/72 inch units.
CHR$(9)	Horizontal tab.
CHR$(11)	Vertical tab.
e	Tab unit setting.
f	Skip position setting.
C	Form length setting.
N	Skip over perforation setting.
O	Skip over perforation cancel.
Q	Right margin set.
I	Left margin set.
8	Ignore paper end detector.
9	Enable paper end detector.
<	One line unidirectional printing.
@	Restore normal settings.
U	Unidirectional printing.
S	Half speed (quiet!) printing.

Other codes can be used to control each pin in the head so that graphics can be printed. This allows 'screen dump' programs which place a copy of the screen graphics on to the paper to be written for this printer.

Fig. 7.11. The software selections of the RX80.

International character sets (U.S.A., France, Germany, England, Denmark, Sweden, Italy, Spain, Japan, Norway) can be printed, and are under software control. This means that selection is done by printing CHR$ numbers rather than by altering switches on the printer itself. The only switches that you have to alter are for such items as are listed in Fig. 7.10. For a lot of purposes, you would probably never need to alter the factory settings of these switches. Figure 7.11 shows the options that can be selected by sending CHR$(27)CHR$(N) codes to the printer.

The Juki 6100 daisywheel

The Juki was one of the first low-cost daisywheel printers to become available. Like most printers, it comes with a Centronics parallel interface, though an RS-232 serial interface is available at extra cost. The Juki is a large and very heavy machine which can accept paper up to thirteen inches wide. The daisywheel is of the same type as is used on Triumph-Adler printers, and the ribbon cartridge is an IBM Selectric 82/C type. The ribbon that was supplied with my Juki was of the 'single strike' variety, and this had a very short life (about three chapters of this book!). A 'multistrike' type of ribbon is much better. These ribbons are very easy to obtain from a lot of suppliers. The ribbons are carbon film rather than inked nylon, and are thrown away after use. This always seems a pity, because the cartridge contains a lot of mechanism that look as if it could easily be used again. Some day, I'll try reloading one of these cartridges.

The printhead of the Juki will print in either direction, and there is a 2K buffer. This means that short pieces of text can be transferred to the printer buffer almost instantly, and the computer can be used for other purposes while the printer gets on with the printing actions. Printing is much slower than the normal rate of the Epson, but not so much slower than the emphasised mode of the Epson as to make the daisywheel seem irritatingly slow. Its enormous advantage is the quality of the type. This is exceptionally clear on the top copy, and even three carbons later it is still very legible. For any letter work, or for the manuscript of a book, the Juki is ideal.

READY.

```
10 REM DEMONSTRATION OF JUKI
20 OPEN3,4
30 PRINT#3,"THIS IS JUKI NORMAL PRINT"
40 PRINT#3,CHR$(27);"E";"THIS IS UNDERLINED";CHR$(27)"R"
50 PRINT#3,"WE CAN CHANGE ";CHR$(27);"O";"TO BOLD PRINT"
60 PRINT#3,"WE CAN CHANGE TO ";CHR$(27);"W";"SHADOW PRINT."
```

READY.

THIS IS JUKI NORMAL PRINT
<u>THIS IS UNDERLINED</u>
WE CAN CHANGE TO **BOLD PRINT**
WE CAN CHANGE TO **SHADOW PRINT.**

Fig. 7.12. The printing of the Juki daisywheel, using the Courier 10 daisywheel.

As you would expect of any modern design of printer, the Juki permits a lot of character sets, but you need to have the appropriate daisywheels fitted for each language. You cannot, for example, have words in alternate character sets without changing wheels in between. Changing wheels is particularly simple, but this is something that you don't have to worry about with dot-matrix printers because the same dot-matrix head can produce any character, under software control. The Juki allows underlining, bold type, and shadow type in addition to the normal printing style, and you can select your print style from a range of at least fourteen daisywheels. The daisywheels are expensive in comparison to others on the market, but ribbons are cheap. Figure 7.12 shows a printout from the Juki with the standard Courier daisywheel fitted.

Like the Epson, the Juki permits a number of changes to be made simply by sending control codes to the printer. These use the ESC character CHR$(27) followed by one more character, so that whatever immediately follows CHR$(27) is never printed. The options include graphics mode, left and right margins, lines per page, half-line feeds in either direction (for printing subscripts and superscripts), top and bottom page margins, and some special characters including the English pound sign. Even more usefully, the print can be changed to bold or shadow by sending such codes, and text can be underlined. Figure 7.13 lists these actions.

Each of these codes will be preceded by CHR$(27).

Code	Effect
1	Set horizontal tab (HT) at present position.
2	Clear all tabs.
3	Graphics mode on (C/R clears).
4	Graphics mode off.
5	Forward print on (C/R clears).
6	Backward print on (C/R clears).
7	Print suppress on (C/R clears).
8	Clear present HT stop.
9	Set left margin at present position.
0	Set right margin at present position.
CHR$(9)	Set HT (tab number follows).
CHR$(10)	Set lines per page (number follows).
CHR$(11)	Vertical tab (VT) set (number follows).
CHR$(12)	Set lines per page (number follows).
_	Sets VT at present position.
CHR$(13)P	Remote reset.
CHR$(30)	Sets line spacing (number follows).
CHR$(31)	Sets character spacing.
C	Clears top/bottom margins.
D	Reverse half-line feed.
U	Normal half-line feed.
L	Sets bottom margin at present position.
T	Sets top margin at present position.
Y	Special character.
Z	Special character.
H	Special character (new paragraph symbol).
I	English pound sign.
J	Diaeresis mark.
K	Spanish c with cedilla.
/	Automatic backward print.
\	Disable backward print.
S	Set character spacing.
CHR$(26)A	Remote error reset.
CHR$(26)I	Initialise printer.
CHR$(26)1	Status (serial interface only).
P	Proportional spacing on.
Q	Proportional spacing off.
CHR$(17)	Offset selection.
E	Underline on.
R	Underline off.
O	Bold print on (C/R clears).
W	Shadow print on (C/R clears).

&	Bold or shadow print off.
%	Carriage settling time.
N	Clear carriage settling time.
CHR$(8)	1/120 inch back space.
X	Cancels all word processing modes except proportional spacing.

Fig. 7.13. The software selections of the Juki.

The same quality of print can now be obtained from a large number of daisywheel typewriters, and many of these can be obtained with a Centronics parallel interface. This type of machine offers a lot of advantages because it can be used as a typewriter for small items that do not justify the use of the computer, yet is available for word processing use along with the C'64 and such programs as Viza-write. These machines can now be bought in the high street stores as well as from office supply shops. The only thing to make sure of is that replacement ribbons and daisywheels are obtainable from several different sources. There's nothing worse than being stuck with a machine for which you can get spares from only one supplier.

The CGP-115 four-colour graphics printer

One of the most popular small graphics printer mechanisms is made under the trademark of ALPS. It's Japanese, and in place of the mechanisms that are used by most printers it actually *draws* its characters with a set of four miniature ball pens. The reason for the set of four is that this allows printing in four different colours – black, blue, red and green. The mechanism is made into boxed units by many manufacturers and sold under a wide variety of names, but it is most easily obtained from Tandy stores under the Tandy code number of CGP-115. This version includes both a Centronics and a serial interface, which makes the printer usable on practically any microcomputer which uses reasonably standard interfaces. Since the Tandy stores offer a good service on spares (pens, paper, etc.) and trouble-shooting, it makes sense to buy the Tandy version as there is a Tandy store in most large towns. In addition to being used as a printer, however, this machine acts as a graphics plotter, and you can draw diagrams and other pictures by means of instructions sent from the computer. Commodore advertise what appears to be a version of this printer (for use with Commodore machines only) as the 1520 graphics printer.

The CGP-115 in detail

The printer uses a plain paper roll which is four and a half inches wide. Tandy stores sell three rolls, each about 145 to 150 feet long, for just under £5. These paper rolls are also used by a wide variety of adding machines, so if you haunt your local office supply stores you may find alternative sources at lower prices. The paper is tightly gripped by the printer, because it is moved around a lot in the course of printing. The printing carriage consists of a holder which is loaded with four miniature ball pens. This holder can be rotated so that one pen is touching the paper. Printing is done by moving the pen holder from side to side and the paper up and down, and it's such a fascinating sight that you'll probably print listings over and over again just for the pleasure of watching the mechanism! I know that I did. When the printer is switched on it goes into a 'pen test' routine, slowly drawing a square in each colour so that you can check that none of the pens has run dry. They have a surprisingly long life, and each pack of three pens costs around £1.99 from Tandy stores. You won't find alternative supplies quite so easily in this case!

Normally, the CGP-15 acts as a printer and you can use it to print listings. It is not quite so fast as the VIC printer, but the results are much easier to read. The enormous advantage of using the Tandy printer, however, is that it can be used as a graphics plotter. This means that if you send suitable instructions to the printer it will draw diagrams. The instructions are not the same as the graphics instructions of the C'64 (or any other computer), but this is not a disadvantage. If at some stage you change to another computer the Tandy printer will still be useful, and the graphics programs that you have used with C'64 can easily be adapted to another computer. This is very useful to know if your household is on the verge of becoming a two-computer family!

The CGP-115 has a small set of four switches at the back which can be used for setting up the printer. For the C'64, the settings of the switches are: 1 OFF, 2 ON, 3 ON, 4 ON. This gives the correct line feed, and the normal size of print, with the parallel interface in use.

The Tandy CGP-115 commands

Because this book is mainly concerned with the use of the Commodore disk drive and several different printers, I have had to resist the temptation to add several chapters on the Tandy graphics printer. Many C'64 owners, however, will probably want to make use of this type of printer mechanism, which is sold under a variety of other brand names. The following is a list of the commands which are available when the Tandy version is used. The commands are shown in their C'64 form, assuming that the command OPEN3,4 has been carried out. Figure 7.14 demonstrates the use of these commands in printing a name in four different directions.

PRINT#3,CHR$ (8) Move one space left (backspace). Used in text mode.

PRINT#3,CHR$ (11) Reverse line feed – move paper down by one line in text mode.

PRINT#3,CHR$ (17) Select text mode from graphics mode.

PRINT#3,CHR$ (18) Select graphics mode from text mode.

PRINT#3,CHR$ (29) Change colour in text mode.

Graphics commands
The following letters can be sent when the printer is in *graphics* mode. The letters are *not* printed; instead, they are used as commands. Several of these commands must be followed by numbers, such as X, Y co-ordinate numbers, to specify positions. All of these letters would be sent to the printer by using PRINT#3 after executing PRINT#3,CHR$(18).

A Reset pen to left margin, no line drawn, return to text mode.

Cn Change colour of pen. n is colour number, 0 to 3.

Dx,y Draw from present position to point x,y. Can be extended to more than one point.

H Move pen to origin without drawing a line. The origin is a specified starting point.

I Set new origin at current pen position. If you want a new origin at point 5,10, then place the pen there and PRINT#3, "I".

Jx,y Jump, or draw-relative. Draws a line from present position to one x steps to the right and y steps up. Do not confuse this with D, which draws to the absolute point x,y.

Ln	Change line type. If n=0, the line is solid, but using numbers 1 to 15 will draw various dotted lines.
Mx,y	Move to point x,y without drawing a line.
Pchars	Print the following characters while the printer is in graphics mode. The size of the characters can be controlled, and characters can be printed vertically or backwards.
Qdir	Change print direction. The number 'dir' can be in the range 0 to 3. 0 gives normal printing, 1 gives top to bottom, 2 gives upside down, 3 gives bottom to top.
Rx,y	Relative move. Move pen, without drawing, to a point x steps to the right and y steps up. Using −x moves left, using −y moves down.
Sn	Selects size of characters to be printed. n must be between 0 and 63.
Xa,b,c	Draw graph axis. n is 0 for a Y-axis, 1 for X-axis. The distance between marks on the axis is specified by 'b', which must be between −999 and +999. The number of steps is 'c', between 1 and 255.

```
READY.


10 REM DIRECTIONS
20 OPEN3,4
30 PRINT#3,CHR$(18)
40 PRINT#3,"M50,0"
50 INPUT"YOUR NAME, PLEASE ";NM$
60 PRINT#3,"P";NM$
70 PRINT#3,"Q1"
80 PRINT#3,"P";NM$
90 PRINT#3,"Q2"
100 PRINT#3,"P";NM$
110 PRINT#3,"Q3"
120 PRINT#3,"P";NM$
130 PRINT#3,"Q0"
140 PRINT#3,"A"
150 END


READY.
```

Fig. 7.14. A printout from the Tandy CGP-115 graphics printer.

Appendix A
Random Access Files

The C'64 disk system permits the use of random access files. Random access means that any track, any sector, and any byte can be read or written. This technique requires a lot of care in use, and for data filing it's always better to make use of serial files or relative files. The only purpose for which true random access filing is really useful is for machine code work, and for writing programs that examine or change the characters on the disk. The reason you have to be careful with the use of random access is that any part of the disk can be changed when this filing method is in use. You could, for example, write data all over the directory track and make a disk unusable. When you make use of serial or relative files, accidents of that kind can't happen.

A random access file is opened by the same type of command as we have used for other files, but with the # symbol enclosed between quotes. For example, OPEN 5,8,5"#" would open a random access file on channel 5. You can, if you want to, specify which buffer number within the computer is to be used. By using "#1" in place of "#", for example, you can specify that buffer number 1 will be used. This is not something you would normally want to do except for specialised purposes. These purposes would include controlling the disk drive directly by the use of machine code, and that's outside the scope of this book.

Once the channel has been opened for random access, and the disk control channel 15 has also been opened, you can send random access commands. The first two of these that you need to know are B-R and B-P. B-R means 'buffer-read', and it causes a sector to be loaded from the disk into a buffer memory. The B-R command has to be followed by four numbers which are, in order, the channel number, the drive number, the track number and the sector number. The result of the command will be to load the whole of the specified sector into buffer memory. Associated with this is the B-P ('buffer pointer') command. This allows a portion to be selected from the buffer. The B-P command has to be followed by two numbers. The first of these is the channel number as before, the second is the position in the buffer where reading is to start. After these commands have been executed, the bytes in the buffer can be read by using a loop that contains GET A$.

```
10 OPEN15,8,15
20 OPEN6,8,6,"#"
30 PRINT#15,"B-R:";6;0;18;0
40 PRINT#15,"B-P";6;144
50 FORN=1TO50
60 GET#6,A$
70 V=ASC(A$+CHR$(0))
80 IF V<31ORV>127THEN V=32
85 PRINTCHR$(V);
90 NEXT
100 CLOSE6:CLOSE15
200 END
1000 OPEN15,8,15
1010 INPUT#15,A,B$,C,D
1020 PRINT B$
```

Fig. A.1. Reading a sector.

Figure A.1 contains an example of the use of these commands. Lines 10 and 20 open the two channels, with the hashmark used to open channel 6 for random access. Line 30 specifies that track 18, sector 0, will be read, and the buffer pointer in line 40 specifies the place in this sector where the name of the disk is stored. The loop that starts in line 50 will then read characters from this point on. If we want to print the results, we have to be careful to filter out any characters that do not print but which might have undesirable results. This is done by lines 70 and 80. Note that CHR$(0) has to be added to a character before taking VAL, because if the character is a zero a straight VAL(A$) would cause an error. It's a peculiarity of the C'64 that can baffle you if you don't know about it.

Now take a look at a development of this program in Fig. A.2. This time the name of the disk is read, and a new name is requested. The name is packed with CHR$(160), which is the SHIFT/SPACE character that is used for this purpose. The name is then chopped to 18 letters, and the block write command is used to place the name back on the disk. Note carefully the order in which things have to be done. The pointer is set, then the title printed into the buffer, and

```
10 OPEN15,8,15
20 OPEN6,8,6,"#"
30 PRINT#15,"B-R:";6;0;18;0
40 PRINT#15,"B-P";6;144
50 B$="":FORN=1TO18
60 GET#6,A$:B$=B$+A$:NEXT
70 PRINTB$
80 PRINT"PLEASE TYPE NEW TITLE"
90 INPUT TT$
100 FORN=1TO18:TT$=TT$+CHR$(160)
110 TT$=LEFT$(TT$,18)
120 PRINT#15,"B-P:";6;144
140 FORN=1TO18
150 PRINT#6,MID$(TT$,N,1);:NEXT
155 PRINT#15,"B-W:";6;0;18;0
160 CLOSE6:CLOSE15
200 END
1000 OPEN15,8,15
1010 INPUT#15,A,B$,C,D
1020 PRINT B$
```

Fig. A.2. How to rename a disk.

lastly the write command transfers it to the disk. Note also the semicolons in the block commands. You will get disk syntax error messages if you substitute commas. Using the same techniques you can alter any part of any sector on the disk. Before you start to experiment, however, you can alter any part of any sector on the disk. Before you start to experiment, however, make sure that you keep backups of any disk that you work with. It's quite easy to make a disk almost unreadable if you are careless, which is why you should stick to serial and relative files for data use.

Appendix B
List of Commands

The list of commands which follows is intended as a reminder. You might like to copy the list and place it close to your computer. The order of the list is not alphabetical; it is arranged in the most likely order of importance, so you should find that the commands which you use the most will be close to the top of the list. As you become really familiar with the operation of your disk system you can remove the top of the list. To avoid elaborate descriptions I have assumed that one drive is used, and that its device number is 8. Owners of double drives can easily make the adjustments that are needed.

The following abbreviations have been used. The word 'filnam' means a filename for the program or data file, and can be a name enclosed by quotes or a string variable such as NM$ which has been assigned earlier in the program. The use of 'f' implies a single letter name. The words 'file', 'chan', 'tr', 'sr', are used to mean the numbers that are allocated for a command. S$ means a string variable name. The word 'cmd' means a disk operating command, and 'dsknam' means a disk title.

LOAD"filnam",8	Loads a BASIC program.
LOAD"filnam",8,1	Loads a machine code program.
LOAD"$",8	Loads directory *and wipes out any BASIC program in the computer.*
LOAD"f*",8	Loads a file whose name starts with 'f'.
LOAD"$:f*"	Loads any directory entries that start with 'f'.
SAVE"filnam",8	Save BASIC program.
SAVE"filnam",8,1	Save machine code program (to reload at the same addresses).
SAVE"@:filnam",8	Save BASIC program, and replace another of the same filename.

VERIFY"filnam",8	Checks that program has been recorded. Unlike use of directory, this does not remove the program from memory.
OPENfile,8,chan,"cmd"	Opens a channel number 'chan' to be used with the file identifier number 'fil'. A single command, 'cmd', can be sent with this format.

Commands to be used with OPEN

":filnam,S,dir"	Serial file, name 'filnam'. The last letter 'dir' can be R (read) or W (write).
":filnam,L,"+chan$(rec)	Relative file, name 'filnam'. Record length is 'rec' and must not exceed 255. This command is used to open a relative file of this name for the first time on a disk.
fil,8,chan,"filnam"	Is used to reopen a relative file that has already been recorded. Only the file-name is enclosed by quotes.
"#"	Used to open a random access file. The hashmark may be followed by a buffer number (0 to 15).
PRINT#fil,S$	Passes the string 'str' to the disk system using file number 'fil'. This must have been opened earlier.
INPUT#fil,S$	Inputs a string from the disk, using file number 'fil', which must have been opened.
GET#fil,S$	Reads one character from the disk using file number 'fil', and allocates this character to S$.

Disk system commands

These commands are sent to the disk system by using channel 15. The syntax can be:

OPEN15,8,15,"command" if the channel has not previously been opened, or
PRINT#15,"command" if channel 15 is already open.

"C:filnam=:ofilnam"	Copies data from old file 'ofilnam' to new file 'filnam'. The old file is *not* erased.

"R:nfilnam=:ofilnam"	Renames a file called 'ofilnam' to 'nfilnam'. After this has been executed, the file name 'ofilnam' no longer exists in the directory.
"S:filnam"	Removes file from the directory.
"N:dsknam"	Clears the directory of a complete disk, and titles the disk 'dsknam'.
"N:dsknam,ID"	Reformats a disk with title 'dsknam' and new ID characters.
"I"	Restores disk to normal. Valuable if a program has stopped with files open.
"V"	Compacts a disk, removing unused spaces. This should *never* be done on a disk which contains random acess files.
"P"CHR$(chan)CHR$(L)CHR$(H) CHR$(P)	
	Positions pointer for a relative file – chan is channel number, L is record number low byte, H is record number high byte, P is position number (0 to 255) in the file.

The following are random access commands:

"B-R";chan;dr;tr;sr	Reads sector number 'sr' from track 'tr' using channel 'chan' on drive 'dr'.
"B-W";chan;dr;tr;sr	Writes to a sector, with the meanings shown above.
"B-A";dr;tr;sr	Allocates a free track and sector for random access filing.
"B-F";dr,tr,sr	Frees a sector for other uses so that it can be reallocated.
"B-P";chan;pos	Sets pointer in a buffer to position number 'pos'.
"U1:";chan;dr;tr;sr	Reads whole of a sector 'sr'.
"U2:";chan;dr;tr;sr	Writes whole of a sector.

The following commands refer to locations in the memory of the disk controller, and are used for machine code control of the disk system.

"M-R:"CHR$(L)CHR$(H)	Read controller memory at address HL.

"M-W:"CHR$(L)CHR$(H)CHR$(N)"data"

> Write data to controller starting with memory address HL. The number of bytes of data is given by 'N' (up to 255).

"M-E:"CHR$(L)CHR$(H)

> Execute machine code starting at address HL.

"B-E:";chan;dr;tr;sr

> Load a complete sector 'sr' from track 'tr', using drive 'dr' and channel 'chan'. This sector must contain machine code which will be executed as soon as it has been loaded. This can, for example, be used to load and run a Centronics interface program, or to make a BASIC program load and run. For machine code experts only!

Appendix C
Disk Head Care

A disk system is such a reliable mechanism that it's easy to forget that it gets a lot of use. This large amount of use involves many movements of the head, much contact of the head with the disk, and it has two effects. One is that the stepping motor will eventually wear out. The stepping motor, as its name suggests, is the device that is responsible for moving the head in steps from one track to another. Modern stepping motors have a very long life, but wear is inevitable, particularly if you use programs which continually access a disk (like spelling checkers). When the stepping motor starts to wear out, you will find that disks do not format properly, and it can sometimes become difficult to read programs at the extremes of the disk. Overhaul and replacement are the only remedy available when this happens. It should not happen, though, in ordinary use, for a long time. What constitutes a long time depends on how much you use disks. For the hobbyist user, it's likely that the disk drive might outlive the use of the computer!

The other problem that arises is head contamination. Disks are clean when you receive them from the manufacturers, but they pick up dirt in use. The jacket helps to protect disks to a considerable extent, but if disk drives are used near a kitchen, or in a place where smoke is present, then the disks will pick up a film of greasy materials. This will be passed on to the disk head as the disk is used. Gradually, the film hardens and thickens, and the eventual result is that the space between the head and the disk becomes too great for reliable use. You may find that writing is still possible, but that reading the disk is less easy. When this state occurs it's time to clean the disk drive head.

Professional maintenance of disk drives involves stripping down the drive to that the head can be cleaned directly. For obvious reasons, this is a method that most of us would prefer to avoid and the alternative is to use one of the disk-drive cleaners that are marketed by the firms whose names are listed in Appendix F. These cleaning systems use a disk of textile material, enclosed in the usual jacket. The cleaning disk surface can be impregnated with cleaning liquid (a quick-drying alcohol) and the disk inserted into the drive. Using a LOAD"$",8 command will then cause the head to make contact with the disk. This rubs the fibre of the disk, along with the cleaning liquid, against the head. The liquid dissolves and loosens greasy deposits, and the spinning cloth disk will wipe the head clean. By the time that the system rejects the disk as being unformatted, the head should be clean. However, if there is a noticeable amount of dirt on the cloth surface of the cleaning disk the action should be repeated with another cleaning disk.

Some cleaning disks come with one surface only exposed, but this is *not* the surface that a Commodore head touches. In this case, you will find that the disk jacket has a perforated tear-out flap on the other side. Removing this flap will allow the Commodore disk head to touch the cloth disk. The head of the Commodore drive is above the disk, not below.

Locating disk drives

Some faults which might appear to be disk faults are, in fact, due to location of the disk drive relative to colour monitors. When a disk drive is used, the normal formatting command will carry out marking, recording and verifying. If you find that disks consistently show formatting faults, particularly refusing to format beyond some point on the disk, then the fault may lie in the positioning of the disk drive unit. Several modern colour monitors, and colour TV receivers used as monitors, have very strong magnetic fields underneath them. These strong magnetic fields will demagnetise a disk, even a disk in a drive a few inches below the monitor. This can be a problem, because a favourite way of assembling a computer system is with the disk drive over the computer and the monitor above the disk drive. Many commercial computer stands are arranged so that the components can be stacked in this way. If you find problems with formatting disks or loading programs, then before returning your drive(s), it is worthwhile to check the effect of placing the monitor another few inches away from the disk drive.

Appendix D
Word Processing with a Disk System

One of the main reasons for any computer user buying a disk system is because he/she wants to make use of word processing. Word processing is much more greedy with memory than most other computer applications, and the use of a disk system is almost essential because of the very slow ràte of saving or loading with tape There are, however, considerable differences in the way that word processing programs will handle the disk system.

Some WP programs use the disk system just as the cassette system would be used. That is to say, the disk system is used simply to dump all the text after the document or chapter has been typed. All of the work of editing and alteration is carried out with the text stored in the memory of the machine. This has the advantage that editing can be very fast. On the other hand, any interruption to the power supply before the text has been completed will cause the whole of the text to be lost. Most WP programs will allow you to save text to the disk at intervals. You should do this for each page of text unless this is repeat text for which you already have a backup copy. A few WP programs will automatically save text each time there is enough to fill a sector on the disk. With this system, you can never lose more than 256 characters, about 40 words. This is an advantage only if the program can also recover text as you require it. Because the C'64 disk system is rather slow in operation, it is better to edit by filling the memory from the disk rather than by calling up text from the disk as it is needed.

Spelling checkers

Several types of word processing programs offer spelling checker programs in addition. The principle is that a disk is filled with 'dictionary' words, and the text to be checked is loaded into the memory of the computer. Each word is then checked against the dictionary disk to find if the spelling is correct. This is a slow business, even with a fast disk drive, and it should be used only where the advantages outweight the loss of time. The advantages include trapping unusual words, eliminating typing errors, and the ability to check for alternative spellings. Typically, such a program will call the operator's attention to any word which does not appear in the dictionary disk. The operator can then alter the word, add it to the dictionary, or store it temporarily. It's important to note that words like 'I'll' and 'you're' are seldom catered for, because many spelling checkers ignore apostrophes, and will present 'll' and 're' as words to be checked. A good spelling checker should allow you to create your own dictionary disks, so that you can have, for example, U.S. and U.K. dictionaries which allow you to convert spellings from one set of standards to another. You can also add technical words to your own dictionary, and build up a disk which is ideally suited to your own use of words.

Appendix E
Saving Machine Code as a Serial File

The disk system of the C'64 can be used to help overcome one of the serious faults of the machine – the poor provision for saving machine code. A number of very helpful utility programs for the C'64 exist in machine code form, and a lot of these are either entered as a BASIC POKE program, or as machine code tapes. In either case, it would be extremely useful to be able to save such programs on disk.

This is generally very easy when the machine code is entered as a POKE program, using BASIC. You will have to note the start and end address numbers that are used in the program. You should then create a serial file, and save the PEEK of each address, using a loop. Typically, this would mean lines such as:

```
10 OPEN2,8,2,":CODE,S,R"
20 N=49900
30 FORJ=0 TO 599
40 PRINT#2,PEEK(N+J):NEXT
50 CLOSE2
60 END
```

This is less easy if you have loaded the machine code program from tape, and are unsure of its starting and finishing addresses. In such a case, a good clue is the SYS number that is used to call the program into action. If you try saving from one address below this number to, perhaps three hundred above, you will be able to save the vast majority of machine-code programs. The test is to load back, and see if the program works. If it does not, reload the original, and try saving a larger range of numbers. You might have to start from several numbers below the SYS number, and perhaps five hundred or so above. Unless you can dig out precise information, as for example by the use of the MIKRO cartridge, you will have to rely on this cut-and-try scheme.

Reloading the machine code then becomes a matter of reading a serial file and poking each number into memory. Typically, you might use a program of the form:

```
10 OPEN2,8,2":CODE,S,R"
20 N=49900
30 FOR J=0 TO 599
40 INPUT#2,A:POKEN+J,A
50 NEXT:CLOSE2
```

you must make certain that the addresses in memory that you are using will have been protected against use by BASIC.

Note that if you use the MIKRO assembler cartridge, you will get routines for saving and loading machine code as part of this cartridge. You can also make use of Centronics printers along with your C'64, providing you have a suitable cable link to connect the printer to the C'64.

Appendix F
Suppliers

Until you have had considerable experience with the use of disk systems and printers, you will not have explored the sources of supply for items such as disks, paper and ribbons. The suppliers whom I have listed here have either supplied me regularly, or supplied items and information for this book. I have no hesitation in recommending them to the reader.

Commodore 64 utilities and programs

Mick Bignell,
Microport,
7 Clydesdale Close,
Borehamwood,
HERTS WD6 2SD

Tel: 01-953-8385

Supplies a Centronics interface, PRINTLINK 64 on tape or on disk. Also the VIZAWRITE and VIZASPELL programs for text processing and the MIKRO assembler among products mentioned in this book.

Simple Software Ltd.,
15 Havelock Rd.,
Brighton,
Sussex BN1 6GL

Tel: (0273) 504879

Software for all CBM machines.

Disks and disk accessories

Pinner Wordpro,
34 Cannonbury Avenue,
Pinner,
Middx HA5 1TS

Tel: 01-868-9548

Supply disks at very competitive prices, with excellent delivery. Very good line of single-sided, single density Memorex disks which are ideal for Commodore 64 system, priced at the time of writing at about £14.50 per box of ten (plus VAT). Also stock disk storage boxes, cleaning kits, printers and ribbons.

Print Supplies

Willis Computer Supplies Ltd,
P.O. Box 10,
South Mill Road,
Bishop's Stortford,
HERTS CM23 3DN

Tel: (0279) 506491

Supply a very wide range of paper, ribbons, printwheels, office furniture and disks, along with almost every computer requirement. Small orders are not turned away, but please don't ask them to supply one £2.10 ribbon!

Action Computer Supplies,
6 Abercorn Trading Estate,
Manor Farm Road,
Alperton,
Wembley,
Middx HA0 1WL

Tel: (01) 903 3921

Excellent range of supplies including paper, ribbons (including ribbons for VIC 1525), disks and cables.

INMAC (UK) Ltd.,
Davy Road,
Astmoor,
Runcorn,
Cheshire WA7 1PZ

Tel: 09285 67551 (for orders – Answerphone service at night).

Large catalogue lists all types of supplies, including paper, ribbons, disks, cables and furniture.

Cortex Computer Store,
At Rymans, First Floor,
6–10 Great Portland St,
LONDON W1

Useful for printers and stationery. One of the few sources I have found for Juki daisywheels, with a good choice of types.

Index

@, protection system, 33
@ use, 18

abbreviations, 100
advantages, disk, 1
ALPS mechanism, 92
arrangement of sectors, 7
auto test, VIC printer, 83
automatic operation, 1

B-P command, 97
B-R command, 97
backing up disk, 27
ball-pens, 92
block availability map (BAM), 10
blocks, 7
buffer, 38
buffer pointer, 98
buffer read, 97
busy warning light, 14
byte, 7, 14

care of disks, 12
carriage return, 86
carriage return character, 54
catalogue data, typical, 41
catalogue, disk, 2
Centronics interface, 81
Centronics interfaces for C'64, 85
channel number, 46
chips, 3
CLOSE command, 49
CMD3 command, 83
command channel, 19, 21
commands list, 100
commands to disk system, 18
COPY, 28
copying file, 28
crash, 20
create file, database, 71
cursor down mode, 84

daisywheel printer, 80
daisywheel typewriter, 80, 92
data cable, 3
data writing, relative file, 57–8
database example, 63
deleting file, 29
demagnetising disks, 12
denary scale, 25
descenders of letters, 79
DFS, 3
DIR program, 38
directory entries, maximum number, 11
directory printout, 17
directory recording, 17
directory space, 11
directory track, 10
directory, reading, 16
disk, 5
disk catalogue, 2
disk controlling circuits, 3
disk drive, 3
disk editing, 40
disk fault on formatting, 9
disk filing, 44
disk filing system (DFS), 3, 13
DISK FULL message, 32
disk operating system, 3
disk operation error, 14
disk sector editor, 35
disk sector reader, 35
disk system, 3
disk system commands, 101
disk utilities, 35
DISPLAY T&S program, 27, 38
double width characters, 84
dollar sign, 27
DOS-Disk, 4
dot matrix principle, 79
drive number, 17

editing disk, 40

electrostatic printers, 80
emphasised mode, Epson, 85
end of file code (EOF), 49
entry subroutine, 74
EOF, 49
Epson RX-80, 86
Epson print, 87
Epson switch settings, 87
error message, 22
error message on saving, 16
error number, 22
error read subroutine, 22
error system, 20
error, disk operation, 14
ESC character, 90
example, CGP-115, 96
extra commands, 2
extra memory, use of disk, 11

field, 44
FILE EXISTS message, 29
file number, 47
filenames, 15
FILES SCRATCHED message, 30
filing, 13
FILING CABINET program, 63
filing techniques, 43
fingerprint, 12
fixed length fields, 53
flag variable, 75
flag variables, database, 72
formatting, 8
formatting fault, 9
four-way socket strip, 3

games programs on disk, 16
graphics commands, CGP-115, 94
graphics printer, 80, 92

handle, 46
handshaking, 81
hard copy, 77
hardware, 3
head, disk drive, 5
hex, 25
hex scale, 26
hexadecimal scale, 25
high quality print, 77
hotline, 19
hub of disk, 5

IBM ribbon, 88
ID, 10
ID mismatch, 31

identification, database, 68
identity code (ID), 10
identity number, filetype, 42
impact printers, 80
INITIALISE command, 20
ink-jet printer, 81
inserting disks, illustration, 9
interfaces, 81

jacket of disk, 5
Juki 6100 daisywheel, 88
Juki print example, 90

KEY file, database, 68

language of disk recording, 5
leaving files open, 49
lights on drive, 14
line feed, 86
list of commands, 100
LOAD, 15
LOAD"*",8 command, 31
loading machine code programs, 16
lower-case of VIC, 84

machine code, 13, 97
machine-code book, 42
mains cable, 3
marker, sector, 8
maximum record number, 57
mechanisms, printer, 78
memory, 14
merge BASIC programs, 40
merge subroutines, 78
MIKRO assembler, 42
multistrike ribbon, 88

name of disk, 10
needles, dot matrix, 79
NO CHANNEL error, 60, 75
number 8 disk reference, 15

open channel, 47
OPEN command, 47
open files, 50
OPEN15,8,15 command, 19
organisation of data, 13

page zero addresses, 26
parallel printers, 81
pen-test routine, 93
pin feed, 82
plug, mains, 3
pointer, file, 56

POKE start of BASIC, 23
precautions, disk use, 11
PRINT# command, 48
PRINT#15 commands, 21
printer buffer, Juki, 88
printer types, 78
printers, 77
printhead, Juki, 88
printhead, dot-matrix, 79
printing carriage, CGP-115, 93
printing to file, 48
printout to directory, 17
protecting disks, 33
protecting subroutine, 22

quit option, database, 73

RAM, 4
random access commands, 101
random access file, 45, 97
reading directory, 16
reading file, 50
reading file, database, 73
reading relative file, 60
reading sector program, 98
record, 43
record name, 48
RECORD NOT PRESENT error, 56
record number coding, 56
recording directory, 17
reformatting, 19
reinforced hub, 5
relative files, 44, 53
reliability, disk recording, 3
RENAME command, 34
rename disk program, 99
renaming files, 33
renaming program, 19
retitling, 19
retitling, non-destructive, 19
reverse field, 84
ribbon cost, 82
RS-232 standard, 82

same filename, 18
SAVE, 15
saving machine code, 42
SCRATCH command, 29
sectors, 7
sequential files, 44

serial files, 44
serial filing on disk, 45
serial printers, 81
serial recording, 2
side sectors, 55
SINGLE DISK BACKUP program, 36
slot in jacket, 5
soft-sectoring, 7
software, 3
speed of operation, 1
splicing tape, 27
ST variable, 50
sticky tabs, 33
storage space, 10
subroutine library, 78
switching, order, 13

Tandy CGP-115, 92
test on format, 8
testing ST, 50
text files, 42
text writer, 1
thermal printers, 80
tokens, 42
track 18, 10
tracks, disk, 6
Triumph-Adler, 88
twin drive backup, 28
type of file indicator, 40
typical directory, 17

unformatted disk error, 21
update file, 51
updating file, 29
upper-case of VIC, 84
use of @, 18
utility disk, 35
utility programs, 28
utility programs in manual, 38

VALIDATE, 32
VERIFY, 16
VIC 1515 printer, 3, 82

wildcard characters, 30
word processing, 77
word processor programs, 42
write-protect notch, 33
write-protect tab, 33
writing file, database, 72